NATIONAL TO NATIONAL

NATIONAL
to
NATIONAL
A YEAR ON THE SHOW JUMPING CIRCUIT

David W. Hollis

Howell Book House
NEW YORK

Maxwell Macmillan Canada
TORONTO

Maxwell Macmillan International
NEW YORK   OXFORD   SINGAPORE   SYDNEY

Howell Book House	Maxwell Macmillan Canada, Inc.
Macmillan Publishing Company	1200 Eglinton Avenue East
866 Third Avenue	Suite 200
New York, NY 10022	Don Mills, Ontario M3C 3N1

Macmillan Publishing Company is part of the Maxwell Communication Group of
Companies.

All photographs are by the author unless otherwise noted.

Library of Congress Cataloging-in-Publication Data
Hollis, David W.
      National to national : a year on the show jumping circuit / David
    W. Hollis.
        p.   cm.
      Includes index.
      ISBN 0-87605-846-2
      1. Show jumping—United States.   2. Show jumpers (Persons)—United
    States.   I. Title.
    SF295.55.U6H65   1992
    799.2′5′0973—dc20   92-11573   CIP

Macmillan books are available at special discounts for bulk purchases for sales promotions,
premiums, fund-raising, or educational use. For details, contact:

                    Special Sales Director
                    Macmillan Publishing Company
                    866 Third Avenue
                    New York, NY 10022

10 9 8 7 6 5 4 3 2 1
Printed in the United States of America

To Lisa and Emily

Contents

Foreword

One of the more perplexing challenges horsepeople frequently face is explaining to our nonhorsey friends just what it is we do and why we do it. David Hollis in *National to National* has managed to do this in capturing the essence of this sport/obsession that takes over the lives of so many otherwise normal people.

Show jumping is unique in the world of sport. Where else do men, women, amateurs, professionals, fifteen-year-old protégés and fifty-five-year-old grandmasters compete on equal footing? In what other sport is the teammate a four-legged animal with whom the athlete must physically merge and eventually share equal responsibility for victory or defeat? And in any other sport does the love of an animal often prove to be a greater impetus in the pursuit of success than promises of riches or fame?

This fascinating book shows us the true meaning of the familiar phrase "horse crazy." Without sparing the reader honest glimpses of the stresses and pain sometimes endured by dedicated riders in pursuit of their goals, David's insight manages to bring us the reality of the everyday world of horse sports. When one watches any athletic contest on television or reads about its stars in the press, it is easy to lose sight of the time, the work, the sweat and the tears that have gone into producing those memorable moments of victory. By choosing to show us three different riders in various stages of their careers, David conveys how a rider's hopes and goals must ride the inevitable roller coaster of a life dedicated to sport.

We witness young rider Kate Chope's almost daily recommitment to her goal of successful performances at the sport's highest level and see how her basic love for her horses keeps her going through the rough spots. We see the effort and mental outlook of Beezie Patton, who experienced the thrill of winning some of the sport's most prestigious events the previous year. We go along for the ride as she concentrates her efforts on teaching and training, maintaining an exhausting show schedule as she looks for that next "superstar" equine partner so necessary to every top rider. Finally, we get to know the perennial champion, Michael Matz, and see how he has managed to achieve what every athlete should have as his or her goal—the ability to maintain a truly realistic perspective on the sport and on life without losing any of the relentless desire to win so essential to sportsmen at the highest level.

As David draws portraits of all the individuals who make up this horse show world, we come to realize how important a role the grooms, veterinarians and other support personnel play in keeping horses and riders healthy, happy and successful throughout an arduous ten-month season. Utilizing accounts of the real-life activities on the circuit, David has created a book that reads like drama, but accurately details the essence of the lives of these people.

Perhaps it will also now be easier for all of us to answer those inevitable questions about our passion. We can simply give all doubters a copy of *National to National* in the sure knowledge that not only will they find it irresistible, but also after viewing all that goes into this life, they will no longer wonder what we mean when we say, "That's show jumping!"

LINDA ALLEN

Preface

On a rainy, humid Easter weekend in 1991, David Raposa walked, a bit dejected, under the grandstands of Tampa Stadium. He paused to talk to a friend about the American Invitational, which had just ended with Raposa not being able to defend the title he had won the year before.

"Hey, that's show jumping," he said with a shrug and walked off.

Only days earlier, Katie Monahan Prudent was in the arena of the Tampa Fairgrounds on Silver Skates, a young horse new to her but still the only chance she had to qualify at the last minute for the Invitational. The pair cleared the last jump and sped through the timers, and the group of riders and grooms at the in-gate erupted in cheers. A favorite on the circuit, Monahan was back, having recovered from a life-threatening injury suffered almost a year earlier, her number one horse recently sold and two others, each familiar and dependable, injured.

"Now that's show jumping," someone said.

It's a common phrase—"That's show jumping"—with uncommon flexibility.

But, still, what is show jumping? Ask most Americans and you'll get a shrug. It isn't often televised, it doesn't draw huge crowds, its participants don't appear on Wheaties boxes or in Nike ads.

Contrast that with Europe, where riders are paid to appear at events instead of paying entry fees as they do in the U.S. In Europe, major shows attract 60,000 people a day compared to the mere handfuls at even the largest American shows. Major corporations pay to affix their names to those of top horses competing in Europe, while sponsorship in the U.S. remains available to but a select few.

Still, show jumping remains one of the most graceful and exciting equestrian sports. *National to National* is about that, about the volatile mix of beauty and danger that is this sport, one that goes largely unnoticed outside the tight community of the horse show world. It's about the men and women who ride and train and groom these wonderful horses, animals that simply by moving can cause a heart to beat faster.

And it's a book about the incongruities of sport.

If Michael Matz could transfer his success to another sport, he'd be revered in the way we respond to basketball's Michael Jordan or baseball's Nolan Ryan. This quiet man, a certifiable hero who at forty is seeing his last years in this sport come into clear focus, would be the respected elder statesman, a step or two away from a lucrative contract paying him to crack wise in a broadcast booth during televised events. He'd have been long since measured for his plaque in just about any other sport's hall of fame.

If Americans followed grand prix show jumping the way we attach ourselves to other sports, Greg Best would be hawking riding boots as fast as Michael Jordan or Bo Jackson sells expensive sneakers. He'd be the handsome young man on the magazine cover or television talk show, the tabloid topic, the face smiling out from something like a baseball card.

If this sport—long and in a way incorrectly considered only for those with more dollars than sense—were like tennis, then Beezie Patton and Kate Chope would be what Steffi Graf and Jennifer Capriati are on our tennis courts today. They would be models for millions of little girls who wanted to compete on a level playing field with boys, just as Katie Monahan Prudent and Debbie Shaffner—the Billy Jean King and Chris Evert of this sport—have been before them.

School children would gallop stick horses on playgrounds and name them Jet Run, Gem Twist and Northern Magic. Those tykes with broad oppositional streaks would ride wooden horses named Threes & Sevens, a Quarter Horse misfit in the world of Thoroughbreds and European Warmbloods.

Instead, show jumpers—Olympic athletes, some of them—live unnoticed in small towns. They shop the mall with anonymity as their companions. They win championships in comparative obscurity, watch tape-delayed replays of a handful of their competitions on cable TV and are better known when they leave this country and ride in the horse show stadiums of Europe. Even the best performances for the most money rate little notice in the press.

Writing *National to National* meant spending more than a year at close quarters with the riders and grooms who rise and fall with the success of the horses they show. While the world of show jumping and its population are considerable, three riders opened their lives for closer scrutiny.

Kate Chope is a young rider, fresh from Brown University and headed for veterinary school. But for a year, for 1991, she dedicated herself full time to the sport. Her goal was to learn more about the horses, become more of a horseman and not just a rider. And it was a time to learn more about herself and gain confidence.

Beezie Patton is one of the finest riders on the scene today, classical in the saddle. Out of it, she is quiet, flashing bright smiles from time to time. Her working relationship with trainer John Madden is one of perfect symbiosis. He is outgoing, a keen judge of horses. Together, they work as one.

Michael Matz is the ruling master of the sport in this country. Many consider him one of the finest horsemen in the world, but he is much more. He is as fine a man as any who has ever ridden a horse. Seeing him with his children, rare in this community of competitors, is as delightful as seeing him clear a fence in a definition of ease and grace.

National to National traces the lives of Kate and Beezie and Michael and those around them through the year spanning the National Horse Show of 1990 and that same show, one of the oldest in the country, of 1991. In between, they weave into this band of nomads who often spend thirty to forty weeks a year traveling across the country from event to event. Florida. Texas. Cleveland. Harrisburg. Indianapolis. Devon. Detroit. Lake Placid. Upperville. Memphis. Port Jervis. Finally, the sprawling sports complex known as the Meadowlands in East Rutherford, New Jersey.

On the surface, it seems a glamorous life. Beautiful places, wealthy people spending their days riding expensive horses. Certainly, show jumping has its share of wealthy men and women who ride horses but who are not horsemen. And, it has its late-night parties, its long lazy days in the winter sun of south Florida and its moments in the spotlight.

But, in all, show jumping is about work. It's about developing horses, showing them, selling them and finding new ones. It is business, and all successful people in business work hard.

What gets missed by those unfamiliar with the sport are the hours in the schooling rings, traveling hundreds of miles to look at a prospective horse touted to be a champion only to see it trot several strides and reveal itself as a plug. Missing are the days of driving, the juggling of owners' egos, the directing of grooms. After winning a record number of grand prix, Margie Goldstein quickly returned to riding twenty, thirty, forty, fifty horses a day at small shows in her native Florida. Michael Matz, the second leading money winner in the sport's history, was in the schooling ring most days of most shows at 6:30 A.M.

Then there is the minute or so of actual jumping in the grand prix ring, banners snapping in the wind, crowds cheering. From trot to canter and the first fence, and then the pace quickens. It becomes caution and abandon combined. It is careful study and raw instinct as the attack of the course unfolds at a gallop. Horse and rider. Fences as high as a man's eye and wide as the spread of his arms. Gallop and finesse. Speed and ease. Excellence mined in the schooling ring. Then there is the dash to break the timers at the finish line, a burst of hooves and the cheers of the crowd, and a rider urging the horse to its fullest reach.

That's show jumping.

DAVID W. HOLLIS

Hubbardsville, New York

Acknowledgments

Only one name is on the jacket of this book, but truly a work such as this represents the efforts of many, and they deserve mention. More than that, they deserve my thanks.

Chief among those people are Michael Matz, Beezie Patton and Kate Chope, the riders who allowed me inside their lives so this story could be told. They are wonderful athletes, fine people and friends.

I also must thank Madelyn Larsen, who edited this, made this possible.

Also to be thanked are Marty Bauman and his staff at Classic Communications. Marty offered insight and encouragement from the outset, and he and Katie Barrett of his staff provided excellent assistance.

We learn from those who go before us. My thanks to Dan Chambliss. An author, Hamilton College professor and swim coach, Dan offered helpful insights from his own works.

I'd also like to thank the many "horse people" who over the years have graciously shared their knowledge of the industry and invited the initiate into their world. Among them are Doug Smith, Dick Higby, Bill Maddison, Barb Lindberg, Carol Buckhout, Debbie Parker and the late Nancy Stowell, all of Morrisville College's equine program; Bobbi Lipka of Bellecrest Sport Morgans in Churchville, New York; Janet Danforth; John Madden; Pam Gares; Twila Slavic of Justamere Equestrian Center

xv

in New Haven, Michigan; Terry Bradner; Karen Golding; P. J. D'Ambra of Grey Stone Farm in Cazenovia, New York, and Linda Connors of Hurricane Hill Farm in Auburn, New York.

Bringing the world of horses to life through words is a delightful way to spend one's days. Many others do it, and I am in their debt. Among them are Nancy Jaffer of the Newark *Star-Ledger*; Mary Kay Kinnish and Laurie Prinz of *Equus*; John Strassburger and Cindy Foley of *The Chronicle of the Horse*; Kathy Fallon and Liz Hoskinson of the American Horse Shows Association; Amy Rosi; James Bloomquist; Cathy Laws of *Spur* and Cathy Kuehner at *Horseplay*.

I also want to acknowledge the assistance offered by other friends who write: Laurie Loewenstein and John Boul.

Part of this book is visual. While I clicked the shutter, it was Bob Kuiper of Hamilton, New York, who worked the darkroom magic to produce these photos. Albert Campanie was an invaluable coach and critic.

I would also like to thank Robin Bledsoe of Good Horse Books in Cambridge, Massachusetts; *The Palm Beach Review*; the research department of the *Wall Street Journal*; and the staff of the Colgate University Library.

And there are many people in my life who had the most difficult job of all: they lived this book as I did for more than a year. It was done for you: Emily Hollis, my daughter; Lisa Oristian, my wife and first line editor; Fritz and Elaine Ralph, friends whose artistic talent is inspiring, and Signe Weaver, friend, horse lover and unending source of optimism.

Thanks.

NATIONAL TO NATIONAL

CHAPTER 1

The Man with the Knives in His Back

Three days earlier, Tony Font could not bend to tie his paddock boots. Now at 11:00 P.M. on this, the first Sunday in November, he was leaning forward a bit as he walked heavily up the ramp leading from the arena floor to the stabling area. A new saddle wedged between his arm and side, a new Seiko watch, an oversized ribbon in his hand, he stepped out into the night air, warm for early November in East Rutherford, New Jersey.

Font had just won the $100,000 Johnny Walker/American Grand Prix Association championship, and he was carrying the rewards of his work, his victory made possible in part by a chiropractor who normally confines his practice to the massive spinal columns of horses, not riders. The thirty-two-year-old, Cuban-born Texan three days earlier had lain on a pair of tack trunks in a walkway of the impromptu tent stable where his and other horses were kept, and had his back, injured while riding, adjusted.

The unorthodox medical intervention had made it possible for Font to pilot Lego, the fourteen-year-old chestnut Dutch Warmblood gelding owned by Bob Lemmons's Prestige Properties, over a thirteen-jump course to win the event that effectively rang down the curtain on the 1990 American show-jumping season. For their considerable efforts at besting

1

the time of Frenchman Herve Godignon on Moët et Chandon Quidam, Font and Lego won $30,000.

Now, the 107th annual National Horse Show was over, ending on the same day as the New York City Marathon, which attracted some 25,000 runners, more than half the total number of spectators who would eventually attend the six days of the National. While Font argued good-naturedly with Belynda Bond, his groom, about her attending the show-ending gala at the Sheraton Hotel, the scenes of a horse-show ending were being played out. The massive six-horse hitches of Belgians and Percherons and Clydesdales were thundering up the ramp Font had walked, their harnesses jingling in almost silly, delicate counterpoint to the pounding of their platter-sized hooves on the asphalt. Tractor-trailers, the draft horses of the highway, rolled in, and modern-day teamsters began loading the equipment that had been used for the six previous days at this, the oldest indoor horse show in America, and the one presenters like to say is the most important in the country. Eventually this night, horses would be loaded, many destined for the Royal Winter Fair in Toronto, others simply heading back to their home farms to rest for the winter, or at least part of it.

Members of the French equestrian team loaded electronic gear for the trip home. This wasn't used to help them tune their horses for competition, but had been purchased at 47th Street Photo across the river in Manhattan and was on its way home. The Canadian team and the one from Britain were also packing. Members would meet again in a week in Toronto, the final show of the fall indoor season of horse shows, events that are a hybrid of café-society flourish and equestrian excellence.

David Distler, one of the show's co-managers, goosed a white Mercedes-Benz, the prize in a drawing to raise money for the show, up the ramp from the arena floor below. Ginny Seipt trudged up the ramp, having finished six days of producing the highlights of the show for Sports Channel USA, the cable television outfit that broadcast highlights of show jumping from the National after CBS pulled out. In the morning she would begin a brief stint on the "Today Show." One of the United States Equestrian Team's grooms, the hands-on secretaries of the horse-show world who make sure things get done, stood in the night air, a large horse blanket wrapped around her shoulders, a wistful look of tiredness across her face.

Down the ramp and inside the Brendan Byrne Arena, named in honor of a former New Jersey governor, members of Michael Carney Music, a New York society orchestra under the direction of Lee Evans, were packing up. Peter Doubleday, announcer and the other co-manager of the show, tucked a tattered looseleaf notebook containing background on every horse and rider likely to appear in an American grand prix beneath his arm and, with tuxedo bow tie still tightly knotted, walked down the arena steps toward the show offices under the grandstands. Don Cush, overseer of the Johnny Walker sponsorship of the sport, offered the last of many congratulatory handshakes. Susan and Ralph Caggiano, owners of 2001 Fine Jewelry and Gifts, Oyster Bay, New York, and one of about fifty-five merchants with displays ringing the mezzanine of the arena during the show, were packing to go home.

Paul Greenwood, the tall New York City merchant banker with a Ph.D. in economics from UCLA, named executive director of the show, was on his way home to his farm in North Salem, New York, north of Manhattan. Earlier in the day he had resigned from the position of fiscal savior of this show.

Everyone was going home, and Maury McGrath was not even on the showgrounds to say good-bye. For the past seven days he had been the unofficial mayor and city manager of this tent city of several thousand people and nearly a thousand horses. He had dealt with leaking water hoses, squeezed too many horses in too few stalls, urged people to keep their dogs on leashes (and was ignored), asked people to move illegally parked vehicles (and was ignored, but had a tow truck at his command) and demanded people not overload electrical outlets in the tents (and was ignored, but had a zealous electrical inspector on his side). McGrath even had to rescue a man who had been trapped in one of the show's portable toilets for some forty-five minutes.

People and horses wandered in every direction. Top hats worn by horse-show committeemen were dusted off and placed in boxes for another year. Show public-relations man Marty Bauman hustled to meet the needs of a couple of reporters trying to file stories for the next day's papers, large campaign-style buttons with pictures of his children on them stuck to the inside of his coat, as much a reminder to him of what they look like as a bragging point for a proud father. The first of a handful of riggers arrived to start taking down the tents; in the morning all that would be left were some holes in the asphalt to be repaired and a large pile of manure and straw bedding.

In the midst of it all, the New Jersey Devils arrived home. The National Hockey League team, which, with the New Jersey Nets of the National Basketball Association, are the regular full-time tenants of the building, were home from a road trip. The foot of dirt on which the show had taken place would be shoveled away and the ice replaced for a Devils game the next night.

Tony Font had stowed his saddle, watch and ribbon for transport back to Texas the next day, driving which he'd handle himself. Putting Sarah and Willie G., his two Australian shepherds, in the back of the burgundy Chevrolet pickup, Font invited a visitor to join him at the post-show gala, and then drove back to the Red Roof Inn in Secaucus. This is where Font stayed, a budget place at $50 a night. Many of the riders, those bankrolled by family money or years of success or those riding as a hired hand for a farm owner, stayed at the Sheraton, the official show headquarters. But not every rider can afford $130 a night, nor can they afford lots of extra help, and wind up having to do much of their own work.

Font drove into the night and eventually to the midnight buffet in the second-floor ballroom of the Sheraton. With other riders, he stood in front of the assembled show committee members, holding a bottle of Michelob beer, a nod to one of the show's sponsors, and listened as any number of people were thanked. Font had a slight smile on his face, nodded as he thanked congratulators and then melted away, back to the Red Roof Inn.

About eight hours later, he was awake and on the road, driving as far as a friend's place in Nashville and on home to Houston the next day. Lego, the American Grand Prix Association's Horse of the Year, made the trip in the two-horse trailer towed behind Font's pickup, the 1990 edition of the National Horse Show now just another ribbon to hang among the many at home.

As it always had, the National attracted celebrities, important, also, to attract the notebooks and cameras of the media, something horse shows often struggle to do. William "Star Trek" Shatner was there to exhibit his American Saddlebreds. Willie Shoemaker, the winningest jockey in history, was there to watch his wife drive in one of the Saddlebred fine harness classes. Joan "Good Morning America" Lunden was there, bringing a camera crew to film her jumping, creating a five-minute spot on the program later in the week, making show organizers as ecstatic as an article by New York Times sportswriter Robin Finn had brought them close to suicide earlier in the week.

In the past, the opening of the National also signaled the advent of the Manhattan social season. In years gone by, the Du Ponts, the Bancrofts, the Whitneys, the Bouviers filled four Madison Square Gardens with their horses for sport, put on their top hats and ball gowns and after the show each night, in later years, filled the Penta Hotel ballroom to dance and dine.

So the Meadowlands in 1990 was a far cry from the original Madison Square Garden on East 27th Street, when about 350 horses competed for $11,000 in prize money. It was even a far cry from the National of 1988, the last time the show was held in New York's Madison Square Garden.

Lack of space and increasing costs sent the show through the Lincoln Tunnel and into the sprawling sports complex known as the New Jersey Meadowlands.

"There's not enough room to longe. There's not enough room for stabling. There's not enough room for anything," said McGrath. "Still, it's better than New York."

However, the prevailing wisdom among many others, especially exhibitors, went something like this: "There's more room for stabling. There's more room for schooling. The footing is better. It's easier to get around. Still, it's not New York."

It wasn't New York because of cost. The 107th annual National Horse Show had opened in the shadow of a $600,000 debt which mounted the year before when the show moved from Madison Square Garden to the Meadowlands. Greenwood, from the old school that says you don't spend what you don't have, slashed expenditures. It was to be an austere National Horse Show, and to most that was an oxymoronic notion. Greenwood's belt tightening had become so unpopular with other board members, he joked, that there would be an easy way to recognize him at the show: "Just look for the guy with all the knives in his back."

Greenwood, slender, distinguished-looking, with salt-and-pepper hair and mustache, entered the fray of horse-show management with some sound foundation. As a partner in Walsh Greenwood & Co., he had been part of a company that had managed $250 million when the risk arbitrage market was at its height. In addition, his Old Salem Farm was the site of twenty-six horse shows a year. It seemed these things would stand him in good stead when he was asked to join the board in March 1990.

"We have an incredible franchise in the National Horse Show," said Greenwood. "This show has a fantastic history behind it, but it has not kept up with the times. The economy has changed but the show hasn't. The world has changed but the show hasn't."

Greenwood became an advocate of planning. One year. Three years. Five years. Like a business, the National Horse Show needed plans.

There had, Greenwood said, been a grand patron, someone willing to open the family checkbook and pay down whatever debt the National Horse Show ran up. That had changed, so Greenwood imposed a strict budget on the show—one so tight that it made many people squeak.

"The National Horse Show is too important and has too good a chance to survive to blow it," he said. "It is the greatest horse show around, but it needs a little bit of discipline. This year we had to stop the bleeding. Someone has to say the emperor has no clothes."

In addition to reducing expenses for the 1990 show, Greenwood expected to have a business plan in place in a couple of months, one that would ensure that costs could be covered and progress made. Greenwood was optimistic that doing so would help ensure that there would be a 108th annual National Horse Show.

*   *   *

Despite the financial trauma, there was encouragement for Greenwood on the opening night of the show. The Natural, the twelve-year-old gelding owned by his Old Salem Farm, with Alice Debany aboard, won the Cellular One and Metro Mobile World Cup qualifying grand prix for international and open riders. Candice Schlom and Wula were second, and Ian Millar and Big Ben were third.

Debany's victory was the cap on an impressive year for the twenty-two-year-old who learned to ride from her mother, Pat Burke Debany, herself a show jumper. In 1989 Debany had taken over the riding responsibilities for The Natural, the 16.1-hand Hanoverian, after his recovery from an operation for a splint injury in 1989. Before winning at the National, Debany had ridden The Natural to victory in the Queen Elizabeth Cup grand prix at Spruce Meadows in Calgary, Alberta, Canada. Shipping east after that class, Debany and The Natural won the $50,000 Cadillac Grand Prix of Detroit.

All of that occurred on a horse that, until a few months before, Debany had been almost too much in awe of to ride.

"He's the ultimate," she said of The Natural, the horse Rodney Jenkins had developed and Katherine Burdsall had ridden to victory at the World Cup in Paris in 1987, and then taken to the 1988 Seoul Olympics. "He's a schoolmaster. He's everything a horse should be. He's just waiting for me to deliver the ride."

Debany had spent most of her twenty-two years with horses. The ninth of ten children, she was one of those kids who just about grew up on horseback. Ponies were a way of life. On one, Billy Blastoff, Debany did a little jumping, a little eventing and some side saddle. Not bad for a pony Debany says was a "Welsh-Shetland-Clydesdale cross." She also rode on one of the first East Coast vaulting teams.

While a senior in high school, her last year as a junior rider, Debany met Greenwood. At the time, she was working for Barney Ward, who also has a farm in Westchester County, and riding with Frank Madden and Bill Cooney. Greenwood had bought horses from Ward.

At the end of 1986 Debany went to work for Greenwood, who also paid for her to attend Fairfield University at night. She worked six days a week and went to school three nights a week. After three semesters she transferred to New York University, taking a semester off to go to Florida with The Natural. She began working with a horse named Tarco, Greenwood's adult jumper, who had some rough edges in need of smoothing. It was on this horse that Debany won her first grand prix in Culpeper, Virginia.

After Burdsall left Old Salem, Debany began riding Drifter, and eventually The Natural.

The win by The Natural over a field of thirty-three other horses made up about half of Robin Finn's article in the next morning's *Times*. The bulk of the sports page piece dwelled on the low attendance ("To say the National drew a crowd would be a grave mistake"), and Greenwood's response ("This year's problem is just to get through the show, and next year we'll worry about getting a crowd," and "At the moment, we have no product to sell") to it.

True as those observations might have been, they did not sit well with members of the show committee. They were as distressed with Greenwood as they were with Finn. The show had five more days to run, and already it was laboring under the weight of internal dissent. It never quite got over that.

Even the quality of the competition in the ring couldn't lift the pall that hung over the show. The puissance, Font's victories, the exciting Gambler's Choice and the race to the wire for Horse of the Year honors couldn't combat the grumbling, which at times even mentioned the unmentionable: Would this be the last National Horse Show?

Font won the $10,000 Johnny Walker speed stake on Halloween night in dramatic fashion. Riding last in the jump-off, he and the 16.1-hand chestnut gelding Lego stirred the crowd with a blazing win. Each time the pair cleared a fence, the cheer got louder, and when they broke the timers, it was as enthusiastic as any that had been given to any New Jersey Net's jam, or any New Jersey Devil's shorthanded goal in overtime.

The evening ended with the puissance, and the thought of a 1,000-pound animal racing headlong for a massive wall with the possibility of not making it was enough to raise the interest of some.

Two young men settled into their seats in the lower rows of the arena before the competition began.

"Isn't this where we saw Mötley Crüe?" asked one.

"Yeah. So, I mean, what's the big deal with this?" countered his friend.

"Maybe we'll see a crash."

These serious students of equestrian sports were denied their hope. However, they did see the wall climb to 7' 4½" before the remaining competitors faulted out. Only Godignon and Ranger, representing the French Equestrian Team, bowed at 6' 1½" in the first round. Both of Barney Ward's mounts, So Long and Wish Me Luck, left after the second round, 6' 6½". The 6' 10" third round claimed Greg Best and Moët et Chandon Santos. At 7' 1¼", the British pair of Joe Turi and Ever If Ever, and Margie Goldstein and Daydream faulted out.

Left for the fourth jump-off round—7' 4½"—were Todd Minikus on Clover Mountain, and Michael Whitaker, one of Britain's famous show-jumping Whitaker brothers, on Henderson Didi. Neither could master the puissance wall, and the competition ended in a tie.

No crashes, but horsemanship worthy of a show that bills itself as the finest in the country. That continued as the show did.

Goldstein and Ranley won the Gambler's Choice, one of the novelty classes that help make the National different from other shows. It was unusual that Goldstein, riding first, would have her round stand. Normally, other riders have the opportunity to watch other rounds to find the best way to negotiate the course.

In one of the highlights of the show, Great Britain won the Nations Cup. The United States Equestrian Team of Chris Kappler and Concorde, Hansen and Zulu, Goldstein and Saluut II, and Best and Gem Twist was second. The U.S., however, ended the week with 120 points, to be named the show's leading team. It was a team chosen, like others for indoor competition, based on the amount of money won by individual riders and not by subjective criteria, as in the past.

American riders were not, however, as lucky when it came to the biggest class of the week, the $100,000 Mercedes-Benz Grand Prix of New York. Seven riders in the field had the chance to make the class even more memorable. They had won it in the past, placing themselves halfway to winning a Mercedes-Benz automobile if they repeated the feat.

Beezie Patton had added her name to that list in 1989 in as dramatic a finish to a major grand prix as the sport had seen in some time. With CBS broadcasting the class, Patton and Northern Magic stole the jump-off victory from Best and Gem Twist by less than a second.

Mercedes-Benz was able to save some money at the National of 1990. No car was given away.

Instead, Godignon added his name to the list of those riders who would have a shot at it in the future. The member of the French Equestrian Team, riding Moët et Chandon's Quidam finished ahead of George Lindemann, Jr., on Jupiter and Hansen on Mirage.

With Canadian Ian Millar and Big Ben in the class, along with Best and Gem Twist, and Briton Nick Skelton and Alan Paul Grand Slam, the class had the international flair and stature expected of a grand prix affixing itself to New York City.

At the show but missing from the competition was Michael Matz. Instead of riding, he and his girlfriend, D. D. Alexander, watched the class from the stands. It turned out that one of the Thoroughbreds Michael had syndicated was racing at the Meadowlands that night, so they stopped into the show as well.

Like many riders, Michael had lost his taste for indoors. Unlike most of his colleagues, he could afford not to show. As important as the shows are, they also are demanding, taking their toll on riders and horses at the end of a season that begins almost a year earlier.

The sheer cost of showing at the National can intimidate many. David Raposa had been named to the Team for the National. Because of this, his expenses were taken care of. Had this not been the case, the young rider probably wouldn't have been there. He estimated it would have cost about $7,000 to show at the National, a fee he said would have kept him away.

Still, Michael had had his moments at the National Horse Show. Nineteen seventy-five was one of the few years the horse show made the front page of the New York *Daily News*. Captured forever, hanging on a wall in Michael's small office in the barn of his Vintage Farm, is the cover of the *Daily News* from November 5. The right side of the page is a photo of Michael and Grande. The other side is another showing Grande on one side of the fence and Michael on the other. Grande had pulled up short at the jump. Michael cleared it on his own.

For Kate Chope, the National Horse Show of 1990 had been one of ups and downs—literally. While she and Hearsay had won an amateur/owner speed stake, one of the three legs of the A/O championship, she had also fallen off in one. She tied for eighth in the other phase with four faults. She finished tied with Dr. Dana Tripp for third place in the championship.

Her win of the $2,500 amateur/owner stake was a close one. She and Hearsay finished the course in 49.36. Jennifer Schmidt and Drafty were second in a time of 49.59. Tripp was third, 49.74; and Andrea Barbarosa on Gambler, fourth in 49.88. A half a second separated the top four finishers, with Kate ahead.

For Tony Font and Lego, the season was over. A vacation in the Canary Islands lay ahead.

For Greenwood, the National had ended early and unhappily. He resigned on the last day of the show.

On Sunday morning, the beginning of the last day of the show, Greenwood sat at a table and worked his way through the Sunday *New York Times*. Not looking for the sports pages and the latest report on the show, Greenwood opened the business section.

"Back to reality," he said.

Several members of the show's management attended a meeting called by the Meadowlands, without Greenwood. That was the end. The New Jersey Sports Authority, in the meeting attended by Show Committee chairman Hank Collins and Sallie Wheeler among others, agreed to take a more active role in promoting the show. When Greenwood stepped down, Wheeler, an exhibitor for many years and member of the family which founded Anheuser-Busch, the St. Louis brewing giant, was tapped to play a leadership role.

In the end, some 44,000 people came to the Meadowlands for the 107th annual National Horse Show. When all checks were received and others mailed out, it made an excessively modest profit of about $40,000. That was a reversal of fortune worth some $640,000, a significant accomplishment no matter how unpopular Greenwood's measures had been. It did not, however, mean that the debt was undone. With each show standing on its own, the 1989 debt had been paid down with reserves and through borrowing. Still, $40,000 to the good was better than $600,000 in the red. At the same time the economy of the Soviet Union had been started on a 500-day forced march toward a free market, the fiscal turnaround of the National was no less a feat. Still, the National Horse Show of 1990 would be remembered by many for what it wasn't rather than for what it had been.

CHAPTER 2

What Is This Sport and Who Are These People?

For Raposa, Goldstein, Schlom and Kappler, the show season was still not over. They would once again wear the red coats with blue collars symbolic of the USET. From the National, they went north to Toronto and the Royal Winter Fair. It was a disappointing trip.

For most riders, the end of November and the entire month of December was a time to rest. Just as they took the shoes off their horses and turned them out so they could just be horses once again, the riders themselves were able to recuperate after a season that had begun almost eleven months earlier in the sun of Florida or Arizona. Now was a time to return home, to vacation, to not pile into a truck or onto a plane and travel week after week to the next horse show. The winter circuit would come soon enough, be it Florida, Arizona or California.

For Beezie Patton, the end of indoors was followed by a trip home to Wisconsin to spend the holidays with her family. It was here, on Christmas twenty-three years earlier, that her life with horses took a serious turn. It was Christmas 1968 that Joe and Kathleen Patton gave an assist to Santa Claus, presenting Beezie and her brother Stewart with their first ponies. Beezie was five years old at the time, and what started as a gift became an affection, an avocation, a career and a life absorbed by riding.

"Even before I could ride I was at the barn with my mom because that's what she had to do with me," said Beezie. "My parents always had horses. I guess I started riding when I was three or four."

By the time she was a junior in high school, Beezie was among the crowd of young riders at the National Horse Show in the Medal and Maclay chase. Riding under the careful eye of Mike Hennigan, who had earlier trained for her parents, she finished eighth on a horse borrowed from Hennigan. The next year she rode the Florida winter circuit, commuting between West Palm Beach and her home near Milwaukee. She also missed about six weeks of school, staying in Florida to ride, but kept her grades up with tutoring. She remained a good student when she enrolled at Southern Seminary, a two-year women's college in Buena Vista, Virginia, with an emphasis on equestrian activities. When she graduated in 1984, she was both class valedictorian and winner of the national championship of the Intercollegiate Horse Show Association.

While at Southern Seminary, Beezie had a horse with veteran rider Katie Monahan in Middleburg. Starting in 1984, about the time Monahan started her successful affiliation with The Governor, she was first an amateur/owner customer, then a working student. It was here that she met John Madden, who worked for Monahan at that time, and began riding Black Gold, a horse owned by Pamela Harriman, in addition to her own Untold Story.

The first major break came for Beezie in 1986. It was then she began riding horses for Pam and Michael Duffy's Stillmeadow Farm of Stonington, Connecticut, and West Palm Beach. She became paired with Medrano, the 16.3-hand Dutch-bred gelding who went on to finish second in that year's Horse of the Year standings. Beezie also rode Trudeau. These horses gave her access to top-quality rides, the kind needed to establish a young rider in the ranks of her grand prix colleagues.

If 1986 was the year that opened the door, 1987 was the one that allowed her to walk through. Still, it was an unsettled time. That was when John had left Monahan's farm in Virginia and moved to the Midwest, setting up shop in Hartland, Wisconsin. It was also the time Katie married Henri Prudent, making Beezie the third rider in the barn. Shortly after, she went to work for John. Competitively speaking, that was also the year that Beezie's stock began to rise dramatically. She rode Medrano and Untold Story in the Volvo World Cup Finals, where she was introduced by a well-meaning but poorly informed announcer as being the granddaughter of Gen. George Patton. The roll continued as she rode for the USET's winning Nations Cup team at Spruce Meadows in Canada, where she also finished ninth in the grand prix, the top finishing amateur. It was also when she won her first grand prix in Memphis on a talented six-year-old chestnut Dutch-bred gelding named Northern Magic. She also finished second at the International Jumping Derby in Rhode Island, second to Katie. The following year was even better: three grand prix victories and a USET assignment when the Team won the Nations Cup in Mexico.

But it was 1989 that defined Beezie, that revealed her total dedication, her seriousness, her ability to handle the pressure of major international competitions, her unflappability. In that dream year she won the $75,000 American Gold Cup at Devon and the Grand Prix De Penn National at Harrisburg, and finished first and second at the inaugural grand prix of the Rochester Classic. Beezie and Northern Magic also finished second at the Washington International Horse Show. She topped the year with a dramatic victory of the $50,000 Mercedes Grand Prix of New York at the National Horse Show. She also rode for the Team at Harrisburg, Washington and New York, where she was leading rider at each and rode on victorious Nations Cup teams at Washington and New York. All of that followed a successful European tour in the spring, where Beezie rode in the biggest shows, including two clear rounds in the Nations Cup in Rome.

Beezie had arrived. Not easily, but she had arrived.

"Most of the people who have become professionals haven't had everything handed to them," said Beezie. "Neither of us had a silver spoon."

John said: "Beezie was never given the very best horses to ride, and while she had very good early training, [Hennigan] wasn't a national trainer, he was a very good local trainer. It shows that if you try hard and practice hard and often, you'll do well."

It was hard work that helped John become the well-respected trainer he has become. A native of the Boston area, John started out as a groom, and managed to work for good people: George Morris, Katie Monahan, Rodney Jenkins. With $5,000 borrowed from his grandfather, John went on his own, first working out of Orchard Hill, a barn owned by Eddie Huber in Cazenovia, New York, then moving to near Milwaukee. When the deal to buy the farm he was at in the Midwest fell through, John found a farm just a few miles from Orchard Hill, east of Syracuse and just off Route 20, the Old Cherry Valley Turnpike.

That was when the Patton-Madden partnership began. She the rider cut from classical cloth, he the self-admitted awful rider but a man with an eye for equine talent and the ability to hone that talent, the combination flourished. He'd find the horses, she'd ride them, and both would be supported by Terry Bradner, the estimable manager of the farm for John Madden Sales.

Unlike Beezie, Michael Matz's equestrian career began late. He may well have been one of the few Pony Club members in history to drive himself to club meetings near his home in Shillington, Pennsylvania. And Michael's involvement with horses didn't begin, like so many, with liberal doses of daydreaming after closing a Walter Farley or Marguerite Henry novel. Instead, it was more basic, a question of staying employed.

At the age of sixteen, Michael was working for George Kohl, a family friend, mowing lawns on weekends to earn spending money just about like every kid does. One day, Kohl was ready to go riding and his wife wasn't. The man asked Michael to go.

"If that's what it took to keep my job, I did it," said Michael.

That was all it took. By the time he was seventeen, a senior in high school and a wrestler in the ninety-eight-pound weight division, he was working as a groom at a stable in Mechanicsville: "Anything I could do to be around horses and stay afloat." Besides, Michael had spent a day working with his father, a plumber, and knew he didn't want to do that.

Michael also took responsibility for his early development as a rider, attending shows not to ride but to watch.

"I had no idea about leads and diagonals," he said. "I did all of this off the seat of my pants. I went to shows and saw I could do it just as well as they could. I just didn't have the money or the horses they had, so I'd have to work harder and find ways of getting those horses. Fortunately, I was never afraid of hard work."

That, early on and over the years, proved to be Michael's edge. Within four years of beginning as a groom, Michael won his first grand prix, the 1972 Cleveland Grand Prix on Rosey Report, a hot gray mare. The next year he won the North American Championship at Detroit, and in the summer of 1975, at the age of twenty-four, just seven years in the business, Michael was chosen to ride for the USET in the Pan American Games in Mexico City. He returned home with an individual bronze medal, and a team gold medal. He rode Grande, a horse owned by F. Eugene Dixon, the man who at one time or another was an owner of the Philadelphia Phillies, Flyers and 76ers, and the man who would eventually pair Michael with Mighty Ruler and Jet Run.

"When I was told I had been chosen to ride for the United States [at the Mexico City Pan Am Games] I felt important for the first time in my life," said Michael.

That was just the beginning of important feelings for Michael. The next year he and Grande rode for the Team at the Olympics in Montreal, failing to take a medal, having left their best jumps in the trials leading up to team selection. Two more Pan American trips—San Juan, Puerto Rico, in 1979 and Caracas, Venezuela, in 1983—resulted in an individual gold with Jet Run, an individual bronze with Chef, and a pair of Team gold medals. In other international competition, he and Jet Run finished third at the 1978 World Championship in Aachen, West Germany. He and Jet Run appeared in the 1982 World Championship in Dublin, Ireland, and he rode Chef at the World Championship held in 1986 in Aachen.

It was Michael's pairing with Jet Run that proved to be one of the enduring horse/rider combinations in American show jumping. Not bad for a partnership that had started on a rocky note. While riding Jet Run at Dixon's farm one day, a garbage truck picked up a nearby dumpster and the sound frightened the horse. Jet Run tossed his head, hitting Michael in the face and breaking his nose. Fortunately, it was a slight that was easily overcome.

Jet Run, these days twenty-two years old and grazing casually with Black Angus cattle at Dixon's farm, was clearly a talented horse, but not one of the easiest to be around. Michael said Jet Run, a son of Jet Traffic, didn't like being close to a lot of other horses, and the pomp and ceremony of, say, a World Cup parade unsettled the horse.

Still, the horse was a champion. He had a good shoulder, very good hind leg, and fit together well. Michael said the horse may have been a bit long in the back, but this didn't stop him from one of the most successful careers of any show jumper. Much of that, said Michael, was due to the attitude of the Thoroughbred Dixon is reported to have bought for about $250,000 more than fifteen years ago.

"In the ring he was a real winner," said Michael. "There was something special about him, an intangible. He was able to measure fences very, very well. He never jumped higher than he had to, but he always jumped high enough. He was a strong horse, very competitive. Very fluid, easy on himself. Great stamina. Very careful."

In 1984, Jet Run was sixteen, too old for the American show-jumping bonanza that was the Los Angeles Olympics. And Chef, nine, was too young.

In 1985, at the American Gold Cup in Devon, Jet Run retired. It was a tear-jerker at a place where he and Michael had won the grand prix in 1977, 1978 and 1979. He was seventeen years old.

By then, Michael had his own place, a twenty-seven-acre farm in

Collegeville, Pennsylvania, a former Quarter Horse racing facility. Vintage Farm is an orderly place, lawns manicured, fences painted, barn immaculate, vehicles washed and polished. It is home to forty-five horses, including the show jumpers of his students and his clients, some young Thoroughbreds destined for the race track and his daughter's pony.

Many of those horses would, by late in the month, be loaded on the massive silver, blue and yellow tractor-trailer for the trip to Florida with Michael. It was a drive he had made many times before, one ending at the Palm Beach Polo and Country Club and beginning yet another year in a spectacular career.

For Kate, the trip to Florida in January would be much different from what lay ahead for Michael. Still, it would begin a year unlike others in the past. She would immerse herself in riding, taking a year off before attending veterinary school to ride, to be at the shows every day, and not just arrive in time to ride in her classes and leave again after, the life of the typical young amateur rider. No, 1991 would be the year she was a rider, not a rider/student. It would be a year of riding horses other than her reliable Hearsay. It would be a year to graduate from the big amateur classes to the grand prix.

That she was able to step outside her other, larger life and focus full-time on riding made Kate like most of the riders who ride in the big classes around the country. It was a time to appreciate, a time of challenges, a time when the rider at the top of the amateur ranks would become the initiate in the grand prix.

In a way, it would be a return to home. Until Kate was in eighth grade, the family lived in Coral Gables. During the summer, the family fled south Florida's heat and lived on Cape Cod, not far from Boston where her mother was from. It was during one of those summers about halfway out the Cape that Kate attended a day camp. Next door was Holly Hill, Patty Harnois's stable, the place Kate would rather have been. Eventually, she began taking lessons with Harnois while on the Cape, and riding western at Gulliver Farms, part of the private school where she was a student. It was from here that Kate bought her first pony, Waco's Image, a Pony of America.

"It was the classic first pony story," she said. "He was nine years old and had only been broke about a year before. I'd get on and he'd buck me off. Every day. I spent as much time off of him as I did riding.

"I remember I wanted him but I'm not quite sure why. Guess it was that he was more of a challenge than the others. He turned out to be a great little pony. He was just green when I got him."

The next summer when the family went to the Cape, Waco's Image went along. It cost as much to ship him from Florida as it did to buy him from Gulliver Farms.

Patty Harnois remembered the arrival of Waco's Image: "When he shipped here, I thought it was an Appaloosa foal, it was so small and scrawny." She had other stories about this pony. At Kate's first show, Waco's Image dumped her and took off, requiring some twenty-five people to execute his capture. Then there was the time representatives from the Jehovah's Witnesses arrived at Holly Hill. Waco followed them to Patty's front door. Somewhat startled, they retreated to the car, where one of them rolled down the window and informed Patty, "That's the biggest dog I've ever seen."

Still, Waco's Image was Kate's first pony.

Returning to Holly Hill when she was about eight years old, Kate spent a lot of time frustrated, sitting in the middle of the ring while other kids jumped their ponies. Still, when she rode the well-mannered, well-schooled pony of another girl, she was thrilled.

"I remember thinking, wow, this is great. I remember distinctly then that I knew I wanted to jump."

More than that, Holly Hill became that special place for a youngster. During summer day camp she'd come early, clean stalls, tack up her pony and ride. After lunch and a swim in the farm's pond, there was a lecture on grooming or cleaning tack.

"It was a great place to learn horsemanship, but it also was a group of kids. These were the kids I grew up with. You didn't want to leave at the end of the day. That helped make it a bigger part of my life."

When the family moved to the Cape to live, closer to the hospital treatment her father needed, some of the young riders from Holly Hill went to high school together at Cape Cod Academy. Kate remains friends with several of the kids she rode with at Holly Hill.

Eventually, Kate and Waco's Image began showing, and Kate graduated to another pony. They did a lot of one-day shows and then the small hunter pony classes of the Florida circuit of A shows. As she grew, so did the size of the shows she attended. Unlike a lot of little girls, horses had not been a phase for Kate. They had hit hard and stuck, and she loved to show.

"At the last year of the Cape Cod Charity show, I remember thinking that it was the largest show in the world. I was walking around seeing all these people who were famous, people I had seen in the horse books I had."

By the time she was twelve years old, Kate was showing not only her own ponies, but those of others who had seen her ride and liked what they saw. It was about that time that she also came to sense she was different from most of the kids she went to school with. Her best friends were the ones at the barn and at the shows. Horses had moved center stage, and while she played school sports—including being one of only two girls on the soccer team—it was horses she always came back to.

That was important when she turned fourteen. Her father, an electrical engineer who had developed the first peacetime application of radioactive isotopes, died of cancer.

"That was one time where the riding really came in," said Kate. "I just threw myself into my riding and my schoolwork."

The dedication to her schoolwork paid off. She graduated in 1986 with a 4.0 grade-point average, valedictorian and tapped to deliver a speech at graduation.

"It was kind of a joke. I wasn't at the meeting when they chose a graduation speaker. I was at a horse show."

Two kids from her graduating class went to Bates College. Another went to Los Angeles to perform with a rock band. Kate went to Brown University, and rode. Like Cape Cod Academy, Brown was a succession of good grades ("There was one C in biology, mammalian neuroendocrine physiology, and that was pretty hard to take.") All the while, she rode the A circuit, showing every weekend.

Like many young American riders, Kate stepped onto the competitive treadmill that is the Medal and Maclay chase. She made the cuts but never finished in the top twelve. This was frustrating to the young woman who, as a matter of course, aimed high in everything she did.

"There is a sense when you're a junior that the equitation finals are everything," she said. "Do well and it means you're a good rider and some see it as how you're going to do for the rest of your life, and that's a little much.

"I had to realize that if you didn't win a ribbon in the finals, it didn't mean you aren't a good rider, and if you do win a ribbon it doesn't mean you're going to go on to greatness.

"What really got me—because I don't mind big classes—is that sense of the judge being there. It's a subjective thing, and if you want to make a correction, you're not sure you should because it will look like you're making a correction. In the jumpers, you just do it . . ."

Fortunately, Kate managed to find a good friend when she got her first jumper. That was 1985, and she bought Hearsay, a horse Henri Prudent had brought to the U.S. and his wife Katie was showing in preliminary classes. Hearsay, then six years old, was certainly not a made horse, but proved to be a clever jumper. He was the right horse at the right time for Kate, then at a stage in her riding of needing to move on from equitation, but to what?

"I didn't like the subjectiveness of the judges in hunters," said Kate. "And I didn't want to spend all that time just cantering around eight jumps. In the jumpers, the courses are tougher, things come up quicker and I liked that."

She learned to go fast, and not just pretty. Then, in the summer of 1985, Kate and Hearsay won a jumper class at the A show in Grantham, New Hampshire.

"It was like a light went on and we started winning a lot."

The next year, she and Hearsay came into their own. He proved to be the perfect horse for her to ride on weekends while at Brown. Careful but confident, this 16.1-hand, gray Irish-bred was the right horse for her to enter the jumper ranks.

"Even when the jumps were sort of over his head, I trusted him and he trusted me. Very much the trier. A quick learner."

This ideal pairing produced one of their most memorable rounds at the Baltimore Horse Show in the fall of 1989. It was the first Show Jumping Hall of Fame class for amateur/owners. Kate and Hearsay were one of ten horse-rider combinations to make it to the jump-off. She was second to last to go. The stands were beginning to fill up for that night's grand prix. Her mother and her brother and his wife were there. The weekend was going well.

Everyone was going faster and faster. Riders in the stands were betting on who'd win. It was a $10,000 class. And the competition: Katie Jacobs, D. D. Alexander, Meridith Michaels. It was a very technical course, the kind Hearsay liked, one that would keep his interest.

Margie Goldstein said, "Just go for it."

They did. Despite tripping badly at a vertical following an in-and-out and a roll-back turn, Kate and Hearsay ended up being the ones to take the victory lap.

"It was just one of those special times," said Kate. "After that I knew I could be as fast as anyone in the country."

There would be ample opportunity for repeats of that kind of class when the 1991 season got under way in Florida. Hearsay would be making the trip south from Holly Hill, going along to help keep Kate's confidence up in amateur classes as she prepared to go in the grand prix.

Going with him would be Ginsing, a horse she had gotten from Barney Ward shortly after the National, and Sebastian, a stallion Kate had bought the previous May and Goldstein had ridden the past season. She'd be going south with three big gray horses and the hope of a sound transition from the amateur/owner ranks to that of the grand prix.

*   *   *

Also heading to Florida—both the Palm Beach Polo and Country Club and to Canterbury in Gainesville—were a variety of riders. It was a group of almost exclusively white women and men from across the country. In 1990 sixty different riders won American grand prix worth $25,000 or more in the United States. Among that number were:

- George Lindemann, Jr., of Greenwich, Connecticut, whose family operates major cellular phone networks in the Northeast, Southeast, and Southwest;
- David Raposa, a rider from Clinton, New York, who owns a ten-stall barn, doing most of the work himself;
- Margie Goldstein, who won two grand prix in 1990, lived at home with her parents, rented stalls for the horses she rides and rode sometimes as many as fifty horses a day at shows to stay on the circuit;
- Barney Ward, Bernie Traurig and Joe Fargis, all of whom have been consistent winners, horsemen who operate their own businesses, riding horses owned by others and sometimes ones they own themselves;
- Charlie Jacobs, whose father, when not riding championship hunters, is president and CEO of Delaware North, a $1.5 billion Buffalo company that owns a variety of airport and sports food services, and owns the Boston Bruins of the National Hockey League;
- Lisa Jacquin, who won three grand prix with only one horse, For the Moment;
- Alice Debany, one of the instructors and riders on the payroll of Greenwood's Old Salem Farm.

Also active in the sport are Debbie Dolan, whose father owns Cablevision and SportsChannel; Megan Furth, whose parents own the Chalk Hill Winery in California's Sonoma Valley and Joan Scharffenberger, whose father is CEO of the Home Life insurance company, which managed Ronald Reagan's blind trust when he was President. Other riders include Marshall Field, whose family name is on the successful Chicago department store, and Hiro Tomizawa, the Japanese rider whose family owns Seiko.

It's riders like these who give the sport its upscale image. Besides, it truly is expensive to buy, own and keep in training a grand prix show jumper. The list of expenses is long. It is not uncommon for horses of this caliber to cost $100,000, $200,000 or $300,000, and as much as $1,200 to $1,500 a month to board them with a top trainer. Then there are show expenses, transportation and veterinary fees.

It is this image of show jumping as a rich man's sport that works against it when trying to market the sport to American mass audiences. However, it is just this cachet that makes equestrian sports attractive to sponsors who want to have their products or services associated with the elite nature of the sport.

Because of this, show jumping in America is a sport viewed by the few. Only a handful of shows ever reach the sports cable channels, let alone network broadcast. When they do, they routinely draw fewer than 750,000 viewers. Stockcar, Indianapolis or Formula I auto racing are also expensive sports, but still manage to attract massive followings. But it is the question of money that seems not to have been overcome in presenting show jumping to larger audiences.

This is in stark contrast to the sport in Europe. There, as many fans will pack a stadium to see a major horse show as will attend the Super Bowl or a World Series game in the United States. Many European riders have sponsors; here, a few. European schoolchildren know the names of horses and riders the way American youngsters can rattle off esoteric statistics of the likes of baseball or basketball stars. When British rider Nick Skelton divorced, he couldn't leave his home because it was staked out by the tabloid press. Here, with rare exception, show jumpers are lucky to make a line or two in the "Elsewhere" box of USA Today's sports pages.

As a result, European riders have the opportunity to earn. The British Show Jumping Association reported that in 1990 Henderson Milton, ridden by John Whitaker, won a total of $361,819. Lego, 1990 Horse of the Year in the U.S., and Tony Font won $98,735, a figure that trailed Phoenix Park, the second-place horse in the BSJA standings with $113,182. In fact, Lego's total would have placed seventh in that rating.

Frank Gombolay, a trainer who fled Hungary after the revolution in 1956 and now lives in Purdys, New York, north of New York City, said the sport in Europe enjoys a much higher level of spectator interest. A product of the Hungarian cavalry school before it was closed, Gombolay said even non-rated shows are heavily sponsored, and it is not unusual for local television to broadcast these shows.

"The entire profile is different in Europe," said Gombolay, who has coached riders such as Jay Land, Eric Hasbrouck and Stacy Casio. "The sport is very much accepted as being very important. For example, in Gothenburg [Sweden], the indoor facility always sells out, and people are there with banners and signs for their favorite riders."

For major shows, it is not unusual for Europeans to travel from one country to the next to lend support for their nation's riders. In return, the shows are made special, said Gombolay, offering other attractions and pageantry for the entertainment of the spectators.

Even in Canada, there is a different outlook about the sport. Harold Chopping, a Canadian rider who spends half of his year in North Carolina, said he and his show-jumping countrymen receive more recognition as athletes than American riders do. Key to this is TV. Show jumping, said Chopping, is a staple of sports programming both on broadcast and cable TV. This is because there are fewer sports competing for air time in Canada. As a result, show-jumping events are televised on a regular basis and sportscasts will often include information of competitions.

Also in Canada, there is an example of what a great horse show can be like. Spruce Meadows of Calgary, Alberta, is recognized as one of the finest show facilities outside of Europe. Eric Hasbrouck, who spent time there in 1980 and 1981, said Spruce Meadows' major show each year is "like the American Invitational for five days in a row."

Even within this country there is a difference of opinion about the sport, the riders, horses and events that make up show jumping. The American team that went to Toronto after the National, while talented, was not a cross-section of American show jumping. With Schlom from California, Kappler from the Midwest, Raposa from New York and Goldstein from Florida, that Toronto squad did, however, represent all regions of the country, something not all teams have done, often being weighted so much in favor of the East Coast that some in the West maintained that the "E" in USET stood for "Eastern."

To many, the East has been America's bastion of show jumping for many years. But, just as the Brooklyn Dodgers and New York Giants moved west, show jumping has spread across the country. The move has not, however, created a homogenized community. Distinct enclaves remain. So do distinct attitudes about those locations. Easterners showing in Texas or Arizona or California talk about the laid-back quality of the shows, while those from the West maintain that there is an attitude of competitiveness, of pressure to perform, when they show in Florida in the winter and at East Coast shows.

Not surprisingly, there are also varying views about where the best quality of horses and riders reside. The top riders in the West or Midwest are as good as the top riders in the East. The same can be said for Texas or Oklahoma. However, there is a concentration of good horses and riders in the East.

*   *   *

When the National Horse Show of 1990 had become the most recent pages in the scrapbooks of some riders and the latest entry in the profit or loss ledger of others, some of the most important news of the show emerged. In mid-December, the National announced that Sallie Wheeler, vice-chairman of the show's Board of Directors, would be named to the reestablished title of president at its annual meeting in January. In another move, Henry Collins III would assume the title of chairman of the executive committee, and he and Wheeler would serve as co-chairmen of the Show Committee for next year's National.

Wheeler and her husband Kenny operate Cismont Manor in Keswick, Virginia, a two hundred-acre farm smack in the heart of foxhunting country, and Cismont West in Arizona. At these farms they have produced a seemingly endless string of champions, hunters, Saddlebreds, Hackneys. Along the way they both were named the American Horse Shows Association's Horseman of the Year, he in 1976 and she in 1987.

The Wheelers also became fixtures at the National, both as exhibitors and in the show's operation. Sallie Wheeler's ascent to the top job meant she'd bring with her the experience, the contacts, the insight, the influence gained in a lifetime at the center of the American horse-show community. It didn't hurt, either, that as a Busch she brought with her the tradition of horsemanship in that family, and the considerable clout of her connections to the St. Louis brewing family that already had a strong inclination toward sponsoring sporting events, including horse shows.

North of the border, the Canadian Equestrian Federation passed a rule in late November requiring all riders competing in classes over fences under CEF jurisdiction to wear helmets with attached harnesses. The new rule came in response to an injury to that country's equestrian national treasure, Ian Millar. He had fallen in July, sustaining a serious head injury, from which he did, however, recover.

In contrast, the AHSA, in December, once again postponed implementation of helmet regulations for American riders.

That time after the National Horse Show was also a time in which some well-known horses died. Thoroughbred racing's Northern Dancer was claimed at twenty-nine by a severe case of colic on November 16. The day before, Alydar, who finished second behind Affirmed in all of the Triple Crown events of 1978, was put down after breaking his right, hind cannon bone when kicking in his stall, and then breaking the right femur when he fell in his stall while wearing a cast. He was fifteen.

And, in Texas, Mazarin V, an eleven-year-old Selle Français, died. The grand prix show jumper of William Martin, the horse died of complications following surgery for colic.

*   *   *

As December closed, Michael was preparing for a trip he had made almost every December of his riding career. He planned to celebrate the New Year in Florida, and later his fortieth birthday, and get ready for the Winter Equestrian Festival at the Palm Beach Polo and Country Club. Maybe this would be the year he could finally add the $100,000 Michelob American Invitational to his impressive list of victories.

CHAPTER 3

America Goes to War and Show Jumping Goes to Florida

It seemed the ride could, and maybe should, last forever. It was one that summed things up, distilled an expanse of time and meaning into less than two minutes.

Michael trotted Nonchalance into the jumper annex ring on the last Wednesday morning of January, the opening day of competition for show jumping's second of seven weeks in Florida. Dew still bathed the coarse, wide blades of the Floritam grass that rolled up and away from the near side of the ring to the sponsor's tent and farther on the group of small tents selling bronzes and jewelry and, of course, T-shirts. In the shade of the nearest tent sat his old friend Bob Freels, in one of the golf carts that cruise the show grounds like the countless Jack Russell terriers that scurry around under foot and hoof.

Michael called to him and they chatted, the horse trotting and the rider turning and leaning over the back of the horse to laugh with Freels, a man who appreciates a good horse. It was easy, like a chance meeting in an aisle at the nearby Publix market, discreetly landscaped from sight in Wellington, a community that didn't even exist fifteen years ago. Michael circled Nonchalance at the far end of the ring so he could finish telling Freels about the horse, a son of Blue Murmur, a Thoroughbred the man in the golf cart has always admired.

Then Michael spurred Nonchalance, and the pair eased into a casual canter, the stride of the chestnut Thoroughbred opening rhythmically in the gait that ages ago must have inspired the maker of the first rocking horse. From the long, white, open-sided sponsor's tent, the haunting theme from "Twin Peaks," the quirky television program that once had America asking, "Who killed Laura Palmer?" carried on the cooling morning breeze. Michael, Nonchalance and Angelo Badalementi's music combined to suspend the moment. A great egret, its five feet of white wings extended, wheeled overhead, broke off and flew off to land in the horseshoe-shaped pond at the head of the adjacent grand prix ring.

It was a careful, unhurried ride in the gentle morning.

This was an early high preliminary class at the start of a long year, a season that would stretch from the record high temperatures of January in Florida to the chill of autumn's waning days and the hectic, demanding indoor circuit. This was a time to stretch, to become limber, to grow to better understand this seven-year-old horse owned by Louis Cericeda, whose daughter Yolanda is one of the handful of students Michael instructs in the art-science of show jumping. This was a time for Michael to wear a short-sleeved polo shirt instead of a jacket and tie, that odd nod to formality other athletes never know. This was a time to prepare, to progress, a time to learn.

The first half of that lesson went well. Michael and Nonchalance had ridden easily, clear, keeping the rails in the metal cups of their fences. Michael leaned forward, patting the neck of the horse that is still filling out, still learning, as it progresses toward bigger classes. The pair stayed in the ring. In the jump-off there would be fewer fences, but time was the enemy, that is what would determine who won the $350 first-place purse, a modest sum compared to major grand prix, which pay a hundred times that much.

Michael circled Nonchalance and picked up the pace, and the 17-plus-hand Thoroughbred showed its lack of experience. The pair clipped two rails, and David Raposa and The Irishman won the class. While Michael and Nonchalance hung no ribbons from this ride, the horse gained experience, and that is what this class is all about.

This is what Florida in January is all about. This migration to Wellington, which bills itself as "ten thousand acres of family values," is about stretching, teaching, easy canters over jumps, which at first are not as big as the ones that will surely follow. People come here to exercise their horses and their bodies, to prepare, to reconnoiter and decide the face to put on the remainder of the year.

About 1,400 horses competed in each of the seven shows held here and again in two weeks at Tampa, two hundred miles to the northwest. It is as large a collection of horses as will gather at any of the major grand prix during the year, and most of the best horses will eventually compete. Lego, the American Grand Prix Association's 1990 Horse of the Year was not here, but toward the end of the Wellington gathering, Moët et Chandon Gem Twist would be shown by Greg Best. Raposa and Seven Wonder were getting ready to defend their surprising win at 1990's American Invitational in Tampa, and Debbie Shaffner was showing Volan.

Besides, Florida in the winter is meant, in part, to be a proving ground, a chance for riders to test their number two and three horses, to give experience to young ones, and to possibly shop for the future. Will last year's green horse be ready for the modifieds? Will last year's high preliminary horse be ready for a grand prix or prove itself in power and speed classes? Will a new horse be found?

All of this makes each year's Winter Equestrian Festival in Wellington and the two weeks of showing in Tampa, including the $100,000 American Invitational, an odd blend of baseball's spring training and its All-Star Game. It is also part reunion. After the National in the fall, this community of competitors disperses. The Florida series of shows is a chance to see people for the first time in the year. Even into February, "Happy New Year" greetings are exchanged as people meet for the first time since the sport's Diaspora.

Debbie Shaffner, the forty-year-old trainer and rider featured in most horse-show program ads for Johnny Walker Black Label Scotch, has been coming to Florida for thirty years. As a junior rider she escaped the winters of Syracuse, New York, to ride on the former Sunshine Circuit. Today coming to Florida is far more than just another horse show, nostalgic or not.

"I have a different purpose for every one. Different horses, different goals," said Shaffner, who has trained such big-name horses as Abdullah, V.I.P. and Volan, the horse whose name appears on the license plate of her new red Cadillac Allanté. Some come to be schooled, others to be sold. Volan, who is owned by Don Cush, whose Don Cush and Associates of Annandale, New Jersey, handles Johnny Walker's sponsorship program, and his wife, Nancy Johnston-Cush, needs to show frequently to be in top form. La Juste Valeur shows only in grand prix and remains on his marks. In all, Shaffner, whose Centennial Farm in Ambler, Pennsylvania, just north of Philadelphia, brought seventeen horses to Florida, more than half of which she said she hoped would be sold while there.

Such sales are a fact of life in this part of the equine world, which in the past twenty years has accelerated its metamorphosis from hobby to business to industry. Because of this, the Winter Equestrian Festival and the shows in Tampa, as much as they are sporting events in their own rights and essential warmups for the upcoming season, are also elaborate stages on which to show off horses for sale.

It was left to an insightful horse trainer turned entrepreneur to first salvage and then expand this winter showcase of horseflesh and riding talent. Today, in addition to fulfilling these needs, organizers say the festival also pumps about $30 million in to the economy of this part of Palm Beach County, about what a good-sized industry would bring to this residential community whose only real economic base beyond sun worshipers and retirees is two hospitals and the local school system.

Gene Mische is the president of Stadium Jumping, the Tampa-based company that stages the festival and the Tampa shows as well as others during the rest of the show year. He is also the man most people credit with creating shows that attract hunter-jumper horses to Florida, just as the sun overhead and the white sand underfoot lure northern tourists. Mische is, in a sense, the godfather of show jumping in America.

Twenty years ago this short, sandy-haired fifty-five-year-old Cleveland, Ohio, native was a trainer. He showed the horses of C. F. Johnson's Fairfield Farms in Lake City, west of Jacksonville. Johnson, who owned eight Chevrolet dealerships in the South, wanted to show hunter-jumpers and was instrumental in forming the Lake City Horse Show in 1964.

That show was held at the local high school football field. Tobacco drying barns, unused at the time of the show, were pressed into service for stabling. About 280 horses showed. A modest introduction to horse-show work for Mische, to be sure, and a far cry from current facilities, which today rank among the best in the world.

Shortly after that, Mische became president of the Central Florida Hunter Jumper Association. It was from this position that he oversaw the shows that would replace the Sunshine Circuit. That string of events succumbed to ill fiscal health in the late 1960s. Mische said the association felt such shows were essential to the business survival of its members, so a new series was started during Mische's term in office. These were held in communities like Winter Haven, Jacksonville, Ocala, Tampa and Delray Beach, setting up for a week often at a local country club, and requiring competitors to trailer horse and baggage from show to show.

To economize, Mische made some minor consolidations. At first it was two weeks in some spots, easing the burden on the exhibitors and making the shows more profitable, although none ever threatened to have overwhelming financial success.

In 1972 Mische managed to attract the fledgling American Gold Cup to Tampa. It was to be the culmination of the Florida circuit. The American Gold Cup stayed but two years, moving, like much of the rest of America, to California. A gap was left.

That year, Mische formed Stadium Jumping, Inc., a private stock company established originally to stage the American Invitational, the Mische-conceived event to replace the departed Gold Cup. Today the $100,000 American Invitational held each March remains one of the premier stops on the show-jumping circuit.

In 1977, with the Florida circuit coming of age under Stadium Jumping, Mische received a call that would change the face of show jumping in the winter. That was when Mische entered into discussion to consolidate the shows and stage them in one place, the 2,250-acre Palm Beach Polo and Country Club in Wellington.

Today winter, for much of the hunter-jumper community, means Wellington, a place that doesn't show up on an official map of Florida. It is an unincorporated expanse of land at the center of Palm Beach County, the second fastest growing area of the Sunshine State, according to the 1990 Census. Wellington is one of the largest planned unit developments in south Florida, a place of walled subdivisions, mauve houses with tile roofs, golf courses and horses. Many horses. In fact, horses are at the center of Wellington, and in some ways are responsible in large measure for much of the development and prosperity of the place.

The Wellington of today is on the site of what used to be the Flying Cow Ranch, a 10,000-acre farm on sand and swamp about halfway between Lake Okeechobee and the Atlantic Ocean. The Flying Cow was owned by C. Oliver Wellington, a businessman and pilot who often rode his range in the seat of an airplane instead of on horseback. Wellington was a pilot, hence the "Flying" part of the ranch's name, and the "Cow" came from his initials, rather than from the cattle which grazed there. The man literally was the Flying C.O.W.

In 1974 Wellington the man sold his ranch to ALCOA, the aluminum giant, and Investment Company of Florida. Then, in 1976 it was sold to the Gould Corporation, a Chicago-based electronics manufacturer that decided to develop the real estate. At the center would be a leisure community catering to golfers and polo enthusiasts. Only a year after the purchase, polo was being played there.

On the dark green walls of the Players Club at the Palm Beach Polo and Country Club are photos of many of the game's greatest players. One is a portrait of a man in a white jersey, "Cadillac" in blue-outlined red script across his chest. On the frame is a small brass plaque with his name: Bill Ylvisaker. Not only was this man the CEO of Gould, a $2 billion electronics manufacturing company when it purchased Wellington, but he also is a name in polo record books of the United States. The sixty-seven-year-old native of Barrington, Illinois, was on the U.S. team that won the prestigious Coronation Cup in 1973 and 1974.

More importantly, he is known in the show-jumping community for something he didn't do. Ylvisaker didn't listen when people questioned the wisdom of developing Wellington and establishing a luxury leisure community on what was swamp and sand at the time, a western outpost about fifteen miles away from the hectic social loop of Palm Beach in the winter. Ylvisaker founded the club and began the process that eventually led to turning some 125 acres of palmetto brush and sand into what is now the Equestrian Club, home to the Wellington portion of the Winter Equestrian Festival.

One of the things successful leisure communities do is to give residents plenty to keep them occupied. Golf courses are mandatory amenities. As are swimming pools. Tennis courts too, if to a lesser degree. Polo, and the image of quality the sport has long emanated, was the ingredient that made a difference for Palm Beach Polo and Country Club. To add to that mix, Ylvisaker thought to add show jumping and began the planning process to create the Equestrian Club.

It was in 1977 that Ylvisaker called Mische, and suggested he stage horse shows at the new resort community. The first was held in 1978, and as Jane Ebelhare, the club's director of equestrian activities, recalled, "It rained . . . of course."

That first show lasted three weeks and attracted 200 horses a week. They showed on what today are exercise fields and a parking lot at the polo club. Polo and the show's grand prix took place simultaneously on Sundays, a prescription for parking and traffic problems. But Ylvisaker's idea of concentrating shows at a pro-horse leisure community caught on.

Ylvisaker retired from Gould in 1986, and now operates Corporate Focus, a holding company that owns three industrial products manufacturers. That same year, Gould sold the resort community its chairman founded to the Landmark Land Company of Carmel, California, for $42 million to obtain cash. (In 1984 Gould had sold all of Wellington but the Palm Beach Polo and Country Club to Corepoint Corp., south Florida's largest developer, for $55 million, also to raise cash.)

Although it was Ylvisaker who began plans to build a separate facility for show jumping, it was left to Landmark Land to do the actual development. Ylvisaker had correctly perceived that adding the $12 million facility would differentiate Wellington and the polo club from other south Florida developments, and attract new buyers. Ground was broken in 1987, and the Equestrian Club had horses waiting to unload the moment what would become America's premier show facility was certified for occupancy in the winter of 1988.

Just as the 1991 edition of the Winter Equestrian Festival opened, another change of ownership loomed. The Palm Beach Polo and Country Club became a symbol of the frustrations that gripped the American business community in the late 1980s and early 1990s.

Landmark Land Company's subsidiary, Oak Tree Savings Bank of New Orleans, which technically owned the club, found itself a victim of legislation that came in response to the savings and loan crisis that had swept America's thrift industry. The Financial Institution Reform and Reconciliation Enforcement Act, passed in 1989 as part of the bailout of the industry, said institutions could not be capitalized by real estate holdings. This forced many, including Oak Tree, to divest of properties, selling them to raise cash to recapitalize.

For Oak Tree Savings Bank, that meant selling the properties parent company Landmark Land had transferred to it. Palm Beach Polo and Country Club was placed on the block. Like many other prestige properties—particularly resort communities—it attracted the attention of the Japanese. About two weeks before showing began in Wellington, it was announced that Landmark had agreed to form a joint venture with Daii-chi Real Estate Company of Tokyo and some European investors. The price was reported to be $739 million for the Florida property and PGA West, a similar Landmark development near Palm Springs, California.

Oak Tree Savings Bank would finance much of the purchase, and a number of top Landmark executives would stay on to operate the properties. The sale would have to be reviewed by the Office of Thrift Supervision, federal watchdogs of the savings and loan industry, and the Federal Deposit Insurance Corporation, bank regulators.

*   *   *

As the calculators of Washington bureaucrats whirred, show jumping continued on the grand prix field of the community's Equestrian Club.

That 160,000 square feet of manicured Bermuda grass, the kind used on golf courses for its ability to take a pounding and rapidly heal itself, was a deep green cushion when the first grand prix of the year was held.

January 27 was a day of record high temperatures masked by some high clouds and cool breezes. It was also a day of record high contagious patriotism in America. Allied air power continued to dominate the Persian Gulf War, not yet even two weeks old, and the show jumping community responded in its own way. The twelve-jump, 534-yard Steve Stephens course featured a red, white and blue flag vertical jump near the in-gate. The jump standards were tied with large yellow ribbons, and riders were given small yellow ribbons to wear on their hunt coats. Even the field of thirty-nine riders had a feel of the allied coalition fighting in the gulf. American riders were joined by Tim Grubb, a native of England; Henri Prudent, a Frenchman, and Cherif Bebawi, an Egyptian rider.

David Raposa and TNT attacked the course like a fighter pilot and jet at war when they went third in the $30,000 Gold Coast Grand Prix, a timed first-round event. The pair set a time for others to chase. And chase the others did.

Margie Goldstein rode Kate's horse Sebastian and it seemed as though they would best Raposa's time—but had the number 10 fence down. In the end Lisa Tarnopol and Revlon Adam won, pocketing the $9,000 check attached to the first-place ribbon. Anthony D'Ambrosio and Minstrel were second. Then came George Lindemann, Jr., and Lari 326, only 0.094 seconds behind D'Ambrosio, followed by his ride on Abound. Laura Kent and Night Magic were fifth. Raposa and TNT, the pair that set the mark to beat, cashed a $1,500 sixth-place check.

"Another day at the office," Raposa joked.

Michael did not show in that grand prix. "Another week of schooling," he said of the wait.

Kate did not show in that grand prix either. She was still getting used to her new horses, and she was looking to make her grand prix debut in a slightly less demanding environment.

And Beezie did not ride in that, the first grand prix of the new year. Her horses weren't yet ready. Besides, there were many things to do.

Unlike most of those coming to the festival, Beezie and trainer John Madden leased a farm about two miles from the show grounds, far from the day-to-day business of the place. The horses they brought to Florida were stabled in roomy stalls, had daily turnout and Beezie could ride on a full-sized field complete with jumps without having to fight the crowds of the school rings at the show grounds. Here, she could also work with students, several from central New York, where Madden's farm is located. This is a side of the business Beezie was becoming more involved in, and one she enjoys. It is also one that Madden said suits Beezie ideally because she is bright and articulate, able to tell students how to correct problems in their riding.

Part of that non-riding side of show jumping is finding the next horse of the future. Riders and trainers become a meld of shopper and sharp-eyed consumer. No one knows from where that next Gem Twist or Mill Pearl will appear, so for many trainers, including Madden, every horse, every suggestion, is considered. There isn't a suitable horse at the festival that, by the time the show breaks camp, Madden will not have looked over.

One evening, midweek before the sun finished its dive toward the Gulf of Mexico on the other side of the state, Madden, Beezie and one of her students, Susan Steele, the wife of Dr. John R. Steele, veterinarian to Madden and others, chased down a prospect. Madden had seen a horse the day before at one of the "stick and ball fields"—polo grounds—that nearly encircle the Equestrian Club.

"What we do with them is a very, very specialized thing," cautioned Madden as the trek began. "Not many can do it. But you always have to look. Who knows, maybe the one you don't look at is the one that can do it . . ." and he trailed off.

Madden was behind the wheel of the black Mercedes-Benz 190-E Beezie bought in part with the rider bonus she earned winning the 1989 Mercedes Grand Prix at the National Horse Show, one of the most dramatic wins of that show's history. He pushed it along the narrow side roads south of the show grounds, irrigation ditches blurring by as he hurried to find the woman's farm before dark. He found it. He also found a Rottweiler with an ill temper and no signs of the woman. Madden decided to look elsewhere, eventually finding her at one of the numerous stick and ball fields that flourish like palmetto in this part of Florida.

Vicki Armour cantered a horse across a vast expanse of green as several other mounted riders rode across the field, and to the fence where Madden stood. Smiling her hello, Armour, a tall blond woman, dismounted and walked the leggy Thoroughbred across the road and tied it to the slatted side of a stock trailer. Then she began leading horse after horse from the trailer, tying one next to the other to the side of the trailer, finally bringing out the New Zealand–bred mare Madden had seen twenty-four hours before.

"Can I help?" said Madden.

"No. All set."

"Are you sure?"

"They're fine," said Armour as she tied the horses loosely to the side of the trailer.

The one horse left alone inside began to stomp and tug the rope that secured him to the vehicle. Armour ignored the ruckus like a mother brushes off a child demanding attention, and tacked up the horse to show Madden and Beezie. She mounted and walked back across the road and trotted the horse down a lane adjacent to the polo practice field.

It hadn't gone more than ten strides when Madden looked away, shaking his head. It was lame on the right front.

Armour walked the horse back toward the road, and Madden and Beezie thanked her for her time. Armour mentioned a trainer at the Delray Training Center with a big gray Thoroughbred that might do better show jumping than it was doing at the track. Besides, the guy needed money. She gave Madden directions.

"Don't tell everybody about this guy, okay?" said Armour. "I don't want every show jumper in Florida walking over my turf or making these horses more expensive."

A fish rose in the nearby irrigation ditch. Madden, Beezie and Steele climbed back into the Mercedes to go home.

"I told you it was one in a million," said Madden. "They give you just enough hope to keep looking, and to keep you broke."

Still, he had to look. Madden is an experienced shopper. He has looked at horses in Chile, Germany, France, England, Ireland, Poland and even in a greenhouse in the dead of a Swedish winter one time. Most are fruitless trips. But one never knows when one such trip won't be fruitless, that when the horse is led out and shown, it will be sound, possessing the critical mix of bravery and caution show jumping demands, and that the price will be reasonable. Miracles like this have, after all, been known to happen.

There was nothing terribly unusual about the way Hearsay came to Kate. It was pretty straightforward. French grand prix rider Henri Prudent brought the 16.1-hand, gray Irish-bred to America as a young horse. Goldstein and Kate's long-time trainer Patty Harnois saw Katie Monahan Prudent ride him at the South Florida Fair Horse Show in a preliminary class in 1985. It was at the end of the West Palm circuit that Kate bought the horse, showing it in junior jumpers in Gainesville and at Tampa that year.

Since then Kate and Hearsay, known as Henry around the barn, have been as successful a rider-horse combination as any the amateur owner jumper ranks have seen in the recent past. He was the right horse for the right rider at the right time. Hearsay was the perfect horse to allow Kate to make the change from the judged, surgical precision of hunters and equitation classes to jumpers, where speed, the ability to jump and daring are more necessary.

"I had confidence in him since that first day I rode him," said Kate. "I can have fun with him, ride him bareback, trail ride him. That's nice to have in a first jumper. He wasn't like some wild thing . . . and he didn't scare my mother to death. Some show horses are so specialized you can do only one thing. Henry's not like that."

Plans were for Hearsay to be the horse to help Kate make the change from hunters and equitation to jumpers. Because he is not the scopiest horse, he was to be a junior jumper horse, a horse to be kept for a year and sold as she moved on to the amateur ranks.

Instead, Hearsay became Kate's confidence builder. The pair became so good together that they continued on into the bigger classes, and even five years later they do well. She may have progressed, but she never outgrew Hearsay. The horse's role today is to let her ride well, ride successfully, maintain her confidence in the amateur classes while she takes those first, somewhat intimidating steps into the grand prix on new horses, Ginsing and Sebastian, an open horse Goldstein had ridden in the past.

At Wellington in January, Hearsay and Kate were champions twice. They hung their ribbons as she grew to learn more about Ginsing's way of going, and worked out exactly which bit was best for the eight-year-old German-bred Hanoverian.

But of all that went on in the show-jumping world during January, what may have been the most important news did not even occur in Florida. Neither did it happen out west on the Arizona-California loop. Instead, it happened in, of all places, a courtroom in Somerville, New Jersey.

On January 28, a Monday, the day of rest at horse shows, New Jersey Superior Court Judge David Lucas threw out the lawsuit that had sent the show-jumping world and the United States' performance at the 1990 World Equestrian Games into a tailspin. Show jumping had, like baseball and football and college basketball, found its attention focused not on the playing field, but on the lawyers' offices.

Debbie Dolan, a twenty-seven-year-old rider from Oyster Bay on the north shore of New York's Long Island, had sued the United States

Equestrian Team, the American Horse Shows Association and three members of the team selection committee over the process used to place riders on the Team for the championship in Stockholm, Sweden. More precisely, she filed the suit seeking unspecified punitive and compensatory damages because she had at first been named to the Team, only to be replaced at the last minute before the once-every-four-year event.

Dolan, Beezie, Greg Best, Anne Kursinski, Joe Fargis and Joan Scharf- fenberger, after qualifying events in the U.S., were invited to participate with the Team at two European shows leading up to Stockholm. The plan was that the top four performers in shows in Switzerland and Luxembourg would represent the nation at the World Championships.

After those two shows Best, Fargis and Scharffenberger were unani- mous choices by the selection committee, which included Frank Chapot, Linda Allen, William Steinkraus and Conrad Homfeld, Dolan's trainer. The vote was four to one to include Kursinski, but then that was changed to include Dolan instead. That decision was again reversed, and that is when things erupted.

Dolan unleashed legal salvos. She unsuccessfully sought a temporary restraining order at the time of the selection. Then, afterward, she filed suit seeking a change in the way teams are selected, a ruling that she was wrongfully removed from the Team and compensatory damages, the requests Lucas refused in February.

In the end, Best on Gem Twist was the top American rider with a fourth in the individual finals. The U.S. team finished fourth.

More than that, those at the World Championship claimed the team ceased to be a team. Animosity flowed like champagne at post-show sponsor celebrations, and members of the squad reportedly did not even sit together at the show. America's equestrian team became the source of gossip at the show, some going so far as to say America was the laughingstock of the event.

Although Dolan didn't ride for the team and her suit was eventually dismissed, the episode was not without impact. The selection process for the USET's appearances the rest of the year was changed, altered well before Lucas could hand down any sort of ruling. It was announced that teams for Nations Cup events would be chosen on an objective basis, one proposal calling for a computerized ranking as is used by professional tennis and other sports.

America's show-jumping community watched closely for what was to eventually come out of the courtroom in January because the suit was as much about money as it was about prestige. The value of a horse that has competed in events such as the one in Stockholm grows, as do the stature, marketability and possibly the earning power of the rider. Besides, most were anxious to have eliminated the distraction and dissension that plagued the Team in Stockholm. Americans were also interested in having their show-jumping compatriots in other countries know the USET for its ability and medal count as opposed to its public airing of family quarrels.

On January 28 Lucas said that since Dolan had not taken advantage of the appeals process already in place with the AHSA for selection to the Team, nor the arbitration provisions of a 1978 federal law regarding amateur sports, the suit had no legitimacy. More importantly, Lucas said the courts had no place in ruling how private organizations select who will represent them in competition. The judge said the AHSA has the authority and expertise to do such things and should be allowed to make their selections as they see fit.

It was a resounding defeat for Dolan. But the specter of an appeal hung in the air for the USET and the AHSA, as well as for other riders, owners and trainers.

While the USET and the AHSA had to worry about a future appeal, the National Horse Show was taking a variety of steps to ensure its own future. At its annual meeting, the group elected Sallie Wheeler its first woman president and began discussing ways to add some pizzazz to the show while not knocking its 108 years of history off its pedestal.

In addition to electing Wheeler, the National added a variety of people to its board, including Bert Firestone and George Morris. Still, probably the most important thing to emerge from the National's annual meeting was the treasurer's report. It was reported that the show had made a modest profit. The 1990 show had about $40,000 worth of black ink, compared to the previous year's $600,000 worth of red. The drastic expense cutting, as opposed to increased revenues, was the cause.

To help the income side of the ledger for the next show, the National committee also announced that pony hunters would return to the show after a twenty-three-year absence. The division had been eliminated in 1968 when the "new" Madison Square Garden opened with reduced stabling capacity. Twelve entries per section—small, medium and large—it was announced, would be shoehorned into the show schedule.

Bringing pony hunters back to the National seemed to be the harbinger of other changes. In a show as cemented to tradition as the National, any change has the potential to raise the eyebrows, if not the hackles, of those involved. People familiar with and dedicated to the show would have to see what changes would be made if Sallie Wheeler was to inject new excitement into an old horse show.

*   *   *

Sometimes the apprehension of waiting, of knowing things might be all right, has a more personal, even threatening side. That became clear to the crowd watching a class in which Michael fell.

It was a power and speed class on a Friday late in the month, a class leading up to the weekend's bigger, more expensive and demanding grand prix. The first part of the course set by Steve Stephens was to test the horse's ability to jump; the second half, as the name implies, was to make it jump fast, timed against the clock. Complete the first part clear, and you could go on to race against the clock in the second half.

Michael trotted For A Moment into the grand prix ring, a 400′ × 400′ greensward of cushion-like Bermuda grass, and began to easily pick apart the first half of the course, riding quickly and carefully. Then at the eighth obstacle, a vertical toward the far end of the course, the ten-year-old Quarter Horse stopped quickly. For A Moment has a comparatively short neck, and when he stopped suddenly and just as suddenly backed away from the fence, Michael continued forward. Not even the man most consider one of the world's best horsemen could check the momentum.

Michael flew over the fence, landing heavily on the other side. He lay on the ground, his hunt cap thrown off, his legs askew above him, jammed against the fence. For moments, he lay that way, not moving, as grooms, course designer Stephens and Phillip Richter, one of Michael's students, ran onto the field amid the enveloping silence. For A Moment stood quietly next to another fence, waiting to be collected.

Michael stood, brushed himself off and shook his head to organize his thoughts. Bernardo Mendez, the groom in charge of For A Moment, was leading the horse from the ring when Michael called him back. He remounted the horse, rode the fence that had unseated him and then walked the horse from the ring, under the spectator bridge at the in-gate and into the waiting area.

An emergency medical technician hurried to his side and began asking questions, which Michael brushed aside with laughter. As Michael walked toward the schooling area, other riders asking how he was, Margaret Meloy trailed at a trot, and called, "Michael, honey, let him take a look at you . . ." Meloy, the AHSA steward charged with overseeing the class, gave up as Michael was legged up onto another horse he had to school. "I love all these kids like they were mine," said Meloy. "I hope he's okay."

Ten minutes later, riding into one of the four sand work areas of the festival grounds, Michael stopped to talk to Keith Brodkin, a Massachusetts man whose daughter Heather rides for Paul Valliare's Acres Wild Farm. Brodkin, like Michael, has Thoroughbreds at the racetrack. They compared notes on their horses' performances.

Michael worked the horse for several minutes and then trotted past Brodkin leaning on the fence around the schooling area. He laughed and said, "Another great start. I fell in my first class in Florida last year too." He shrugged his grass-stained shoulders, a smile filled his deeply tanned face and then he moved the horse into a canter to prepare it for the next class.

Paul Greenwood at the 1990 National Horse Show.

William Steinkraus, left, and Frank Chapot, center, chat with Canadian chef d'equipe Thomas Gayford at the National Horse Show of 1990.

Katie Monahan Prudent and son Adam at the National Horse Show, 1990.

Margie Goldstein and Daydream clear the puissance wall at the National Horse Show of 1990.

Hap Hansen and Chris Kappler at the National Horse Show of 1990.

Margie Goldstein, left, and Kate Chope discuss strategy while walking the course during the Winter Equestrian Festival in Wellington, Florida, January 1991.

Beezie Patton.

Michael Matz and Ingliss Leslie, son of Matz's veterinarian, check out the competition during the annual lead-line class at the Winter Equestrian Festival in Wellington, Florida.

Kate Chope and Hearsay at the Winter Equestrian Festival in Wellington, Florida.

Kate Chope schooling Ginsing at the Winter Equestrian Festival in Wellington, Florida.

Michael Matz and Caribe at the Winter Equestrian Festival in Wellington, Florida.

Course officials, a groom and another rider run to help Michael Matz after he fell during his first class at the 1991 Winter Equestrian Festival in Wellington, Florida. It was the second year in a row that he fell during his first class at the show.

Beezie Patton and Grand Up negotiate the course during a class at the Tampa Fairgrounds in Florida, March 1991.

Michael Matz and Irish show jumping star Eddie Macken chat during the Winter Equestrian Festival of 1991 in Wellington, Florida. The two rode against each other in the World Championships in the early 1970s.

Michael Matz and Heisman enter Tampa Stadium for the American Invitational, March 1991.

Michael Matz and Heisman clear the water jump at the American Invitational in Tampa Stadium, 1991.

Margie Goldstein and Saluut II clear the second half of the Shamu combination during the American Invitational in Tampa Stadium, March 1991.

Tony Font and Lego at the American Invitational of 1991 in Tampa Stadium.

George Lindemann Jr. and Threes And Sevens on their way to victory at the American Invitational in Tampa Stadium, March 1991.

Gene Mische, president of Stadium Jumping, which
stages the Winter Equestrian Festival and other shows.

Amateur owner Barb Wolfe, left, chats with Terry Bradner, John Madden and Beezie Patton
during the Winter Equestrian Festival in Wellington, Florida.

Kate Chope, Margie Goldstein, Barney Ward and his son McLain before a class at the Winter Equestrian Festival in Wellington, Florida.

Greg Best and Gem Twist at the Tampa Fairgrounds in March of 1991. The pair didn't qualify for the American Invitational.

CHAPTER 4

Interrupted Fun

On a sun-filled, casual, midweek day in February, Buddy Brown walked Elan's Ten Fold around the outside of a crowded exercise ring at the Equestrian Club of the Palm Beach Polo and Country Club. Walking along one side of the ring, he spotted a friend.

"How'd you do in the classic last week?" he said to a man.

"I was clear and had two faults in the jump-off," replied Peter Wetherhill, an adult amateur jumper rider from New Town Square, Pennsylvania.

"But did you have fun?" asked Brown, who rode for the U.S. in the 1976 Summer Olympics at Montreal. "That's the point of doing it."

Wetherhill, who showed as a junior, then took fifteen years off before returning to jumpers the previous fall on a horse named Eddie Murphy, smiled and nodded. Brown nodded back and walked Elan's Ten Fold around the ring, and Wetherhill wandered off to watch a class.

Fun.

At times, that seems an alien subject at this level of competition. This is business. This is work. Serious business and hard work, grooms and riders rising hours before dawn and working until well after the sun has vanished, trying to show their horses to the best of their ability, thereby enhancing the worth of the animals and keeping the horses' owners happy. Fun and business, too often, are water and oil.

51

Still, elements of fun are exposed. Riders lounge at the in-gate and laugh. They kibitz, some engage in good-natured wagering on the performance of other riders and compare notes on everything from their horses to their golf games. In Florida in February, even as the Persian Gulf War went to ground and swiftly ended, there was room for some laughter and the occasional practical joke. Riders even were able to joke about bad rounds in preliminary and modified classes; they smiled tightly if it was a classic or grand prix in which they went awry.

But, this February in particular, that good humor was tempered in part by an incident that did not even occur in Wellington, this 10,000 acres of family values, and what appears to be at least a horse per acre. It was something that set the show, in part, on the defensive and the show-jumping community on edge.

In the modest press room of the gray, double-wide manufactured building that is headquarters to the horse show hung typed instructions about what to say should someone answer the phone and find a reporter lurking on the other end. The memo said:

> Questions may arise about the possible involvement of exhibitors in an alleged ring which injures and/or kills horses to collect insurance money.
>
> Should any phone calls come in on this subject, they should be directed to Marty Bauman or Kim Tudor. If neither is available, please direct the call to Gene [Mische].
>
> On the subject, Gene Mische, chairman of the Winter Equestrian Festival, has issued the following statement: "We have heard the allegations regarding the alleged acts of violence to horses for insurance purposes. We find these charges appalling and difficult to believe. The well-being of horses at the Winter Equestrian Festival, and of horses everywhere, is our primary concern. We offer our total cooperation with the police and FBI in any investigation they may choose to conduct and should there be any truth to these allegations, we hope the investigations will lead to the arrest of anyone involved."

Also posted prominently around the show grounds were copies of the American Horse Shows Association's Statement of Principles. This code includes numerous commitments to the welfare of horses, requiring they be treated with ". . . the kindness, respect, and compassion they deserve and never be subjected to mistreatment."

These commitments to ethical treatment of horses took on added meaning when held next to the horse-show management's memo about people conspiring to deliberately injure horses.

But as the Winter Equestrian Festival settled into its fullest month of activity, there was an undercurrent of unease. To the north, in Gainesville, a horse that was headed to Wellington and laying over at another show facility was said to have been deliberately injured and had to be destroyed. The details of the case spread through the show community in Wellington like a virulent case of strangles, implicating the wife of one of the sport's leading riders who was competing at Wellington.

Canterbury, Florida's Equestrian Showplace, is a private facility. It opened in Gainesville during the fall of 1990, and in the winter of 1991 it was host to the Horse Shows In The Sun (HITS) series of hunter-jumper shows staged by the Davis group of Thomasville, Georgia. It was there that investigators from the Florida Department of Agriculture and Consumer Services watched as two men set in motion something that would occupy the gossip of grooms and speculation of riders and the consternation of most everyone in the hunter-jumper fraternity.

On February 2, Lt. John O'Brien and other Florida agriculture officers watched as Harlow Arley, a groom, held Streetwise, a seven-year-old show jumper, while Tommy Burns, also known as Timmy Robert Ray, used a crowbar to break the horse's right rear leg. With one quick, powerful blow, Burns struck the horse, and Streetwise bolted from the trailer onto which it was being loaded, running into the night.

Carlie Ferguson, who with partner Wendy Low-Touche owns Canterbury, was working late that night, trying to get the hookups for recreational vehicles working properly. While she and some maintenance men labored, a man ran up to them and said a horse had gotten loose. They joined the search, not knowing Streetwise was running scared from its handlers, the men it trusted, men who had coldly betrayed that trust and deliberately broken its leg.

"It was the worst night of my life," said Ferguson, who originally designed the 212-acre Canterbury as a class project while she was an animal science major at the University of Florida. "For some reason these idiots chose our facility to do this."

She was among the first to eventually get to the horse. It was her call that summoned the veterinarian who destroyed the crippled horse the next morning with a lethal injection.

As the story filtered out of Canterbury through the media, it was learned that Streetwise, ironically known as Buddy, was owned by Donna

Brown, wife of show jumper Buddy Brown. Although she was not charged, it was widely reported that Donna Brown had paid Arley and Burns $5,000 to wield the crowbar across the leg of the horse. The horse was insured for $100,000, and Donna Brown's name was on that insurance policy. It spread quickly that this was a breakthrough in a nationwide insurance fraud scam.

Arley and Burns, both of the Chicago area, were arrested and taken to the Alachua County Jail. Burns was charged with felony cruelty to animals, grand larceny and hauling animals without a license. Arley was charged with cruelty to animals. Burns, through a bail bondsman, met his $100,000 bail and was released. Arley remained in jail.

A near-communal sense of horror was reflected by comments of the riders at Wellington. Professionals, even those jaded by years in the industry, were as aghast as a horse-crazy child when talking about what had happened to Streetwise. Most shook their heads. One veterinarian who had seen just about everything that can happen to a horse said the two could not be hanged high enough for what they did. And most worried secretly that this was the kind of thing that would bring the wrath of the increasingly vocal animal rights movement to bear on American show jumping. This was the first time such a case had reached headline status outside equine publications. It also prompted calls to the American Horse Shows Association from concerned parents, worried their children would be exposed to such individuals when they went to shows. Simply, when Streetwise had his leg broken, American show jumping had its eye blackened.

Still, the sad ending of Streetwise was an aberration, shocking but isolated. Horses, other than those being sent for slaughter, as a rule are not killed for profit.

However, the normal physical demands on horses at the Winter Equestrian Festival and shows like it can take tolls of their own. Such injuries certainly are far less cruel than a crowbar across a leg, but still can be painful and even debilitating in their own way. Notwithstanding the high level of care administered to these mostly expensive horses, injury and illness are part of their lives. They are, after all, athletes, and like even the best, most well conditioned human performers, they can be hurt or fall ill. And, asking a 1,200-pound animal to gallop headlong toward and then over a five-foot-high fence carries some inherent risk to life and limb, no matter how well trained and conditioned the horse or experienced and skillful the rider. It is a fact of life that while show jumping does not mercilessly chew up horses the way racing does, sometimes horses get hurt, and the sport is strenuous.

February is the time some of these injuries begin to appear. By this time the horses have been in Florida long enough to be well into the schedule of shows. The attendant repetitions of training and showing extract their prices. For some, even the simple trip from north to south to arrive at the show can cause problems.

As the official veterinarian for the Winter Equestrian Festival and other shows, Dr. Tim Cordes had seen just about every imaginable illness and injury that can befall horses. Some are minor and to be expected. Others are a result of the facilities, while others can be attributed to the rigorous schedule of shows that occur nearly back to back from the end of January through the first of April.

Cordes, who traveled to Florida and other shows from his practice in west central New Jersey, sat in his office at the showgrounds in Wellington. He had just finished reviewing numerous X rays with the new owner of a jumper, an initiate to this community, one worried about what she saw in the gray areas of the films Cordes held up to the small lightbox attached to his office wall. Her horse had a joint injury, one being treated with expensive injections, an injury that could be helped. She left, reassured but still somewhat apprehensive, thanking Cordes for his lengthy explanation on the inner workings of horses' joints.

That particular horse fit into the fourth and final phase of Cordes's explanation of what the animals go through during their stay at the Winter Equestrian Festival. It would see no more jumping this month and would skip the Tampa edition of the festival as well.

Getting to Florida is the first phase of health change for these horses, said Cordes. He said the act of loading horses onto a tractor-trailer rig or into the back of a two-horse trailer hauled behind a pickup truck and heading south on an interstate highway can be hazardous to their health.

"Shipping down, they go from a cold, dry environment to suddenly a warm moist environment," he said. "That's the recipe for pneumonia, bronchopneumonia and pleurisy."

It was nearly the end of February, and Cordes said he was still treating the respiratory problems of one horse that had arrived ill in early January. Cordes had already drained four gallons of fluid from the right side of the horse's chest, and his ministrations continued. Because of just this sort of ailment, many riders and trainers will ship horses to Florida early, sometimes as much as a month before the competitions begin, in order to give them time to be treated for climate-change illness and to adjust to the warmer weather.

Ginsing's arrival in Florida brought some minor health problems and a new nickname. Shortly after Kate's horse arrived from Cape Cod, it developed large bumps over much of its body, mosquito bites. The bites, common for many of the horses shipping into the near-tropical environs of Wellington, were, by the end of February, reduced to small hairless patches. However, the attack of mosquitoes left Ginsing—a majestic-looking gray with a noble carriage and royal bearing—with a new nickname: Lumpy. Tammy hung that on him while she treated his insect bites.

Ginsing's problems are not uncommon, said Cordes. While the heat of south Florida is good for the horse's musculoskeletal system, it can allow fungus and bacteria to cause skin problems, "And if you can't get tack on a horse you can't show it."

Once in Florida and allowed to adjust, work begins. Some horses must get back into competitive trim after a month to six weeks of rest and recuperation from the demands of the fall indoor season. Others, young horses, must receive some final polishing before their first go on Florida's demanding winter circuit.

This leads to the second of Cordes's four phases, the sports performance phase. This is the training, the conditioning, the preparing. While injuries occur at this time, Cordes said the horses must also make adjustments to some basic changes in their daily regimen. The water at the showgrounds has a high sulfur content, and some horses refuse to drink. Others turn up their noses at the hay, considered by many to be inferior to the lowest grade forage they may be used to back in their northern home barns.

Because of these things, grooms, trainers and riders come up with ways to speed the adjustment, make the food and water more palatable. Such machinations are necessary, for hay and water fuel these equine athletes, and just as a human athlete cannot perform at his or her best when not properly nourished, neither can these hunters and jumpers.

Another seemingly basic consideration figures into the second stage of things Cordes and the other practitioners who travel to Florida with their clients must worry about: the ground, footing in the rings where horses exercise and compete. If a poll of riders was taken to determine the number-one concern about the infrastructure of shows, the overwhelming interest would be in footing. Just as the drivers of high-tech, high-speed race cars worry about the condition of the track on which they drive, riders and trainers worry about the ground under the hooves of their horses for the same reason. They are worried about it for the safety of the animal and themselves, and whether it will allow horses to be competitive.

There are companies that do nothing but concern themselves with creating the proper footing in arenas and rings, and make top dollar doing so. It cost $100,000 for the footing at the National Horse Show in 1989. Managers of farms these and other horses inhabit may use anything from the sand from river bottoms to wood chips to manure from the horses's stalls to the finely diced rubber of recycled automobile tires to create the ideal footing for the horses. The search for and the maintenance of the ideal arena footing material may not be Grail-like, but it consumes the time of many in the horse industry.

Wellington and the Palm Beach Polo and Country Club are built on sand. Lots of sand. Even more than lots. This is the footing in the exercise rings, and all of the competitive rings with the exception of the grand prix field and the adjacent jumper annex. While the sand may be soft and somewhat forgiving, it also strains the horse to work in it.

Footing, though, is a given, something with which to be dealt. Likewise, said Cordes, are the stresses that must be treated as horses go about their business of showing. This is the third phase, the one of ongoing maintenance. Cordes said this is made more demanding by the schedule of the Florida circuit.

"If you look at any other period of time, I don't think there is a more intense length of time, both in terms of having the best horses competing one against the other and the length of time," said Cordes. There is a ten-week period of showing with "a so-called rest period" between Wellington and Tampa, said Cordes, and that is a demanding time on horses and the people who show and tend to them.

Cordes, as he spoke, was in that phase of the horse show's life in Florida. The daily living at the show, in Florida or elsewhere, can be difficult on the horses, and by the end of February Cordes has seen just about everything it can deliver.

"You have a horse that comes from a million-dollar barn and here they are in a tent," said Cordes about the stabling of most of the horses showing in Wellington. "So, they catch an eyelid on the stall wall or the horse reaches over from the next stall and comes crashing through the wood planks. These are things we accept."

These things, coupled with the rigors of frequent showing in arguably the most competitive situation of the season, have Cordes and other practitioners treating a lot of horses. Much of their work centers on the aches and pains of competition, muscle soreness, tendon soreness.

"In most aspects, the vets here are like team physicians for the Chicago Bears," said Cordes, borrowing an analogy from the National Football League. "But an old Chicago Bears team."

Most of the horses competing at this level have some years of competition behind them. And, fortunately, many did not begin the physically demanding rigors of showing until after their bodies were fairly well developed. This is, at least in part, a function of the growing number of European-bred horses in the grand prix ranks, and they come from a different equine training culture.

"The Europeans really have the ticket," said Cordes. "They do not even think of jumping a horse before they are five. Most of the big grand prix horses are older horses, so you're not talking about the two-year-old at the racetrack who's fracturing his sesamoid. It's more likely that you're talking about the older, more mature horse, and the bottom line is you have a horse that is going to have joint pain."

Finally, said Cordes, there is the fourth and last phase, the tired phase, the end-of-February feeling of horses worn out by the grind of a demanding schedule. By then the severely injured have already gone home, skipping the trip to Tampa. In the horses remaining, Cordes and other vets see dehydration, sore muscles, sore tendons, suspensories strained by working in the deep sand. By late in the month, there have been five weeks of competition, five weeks of big classes in the hot Florida sun. That is, for some horsemen, too long, and too much.

*   *   *

Too, it is in February that competition in Florida reaches its peak. The warmup that is January is behind the horses and riders, the rigors of shipping past, the adjustment to the South done. There would be weekdays of smaller classes, Saturdays of big amateur classes and the Winter Equestrian Festival Challenge, big classes for horses not going in the Sunday grand prix. Only Mondays offer respite. Beyond that, the Winter Equestrian Festival settles into its routine, one that is demanding for the horses, the riders and the grooms. The idyllic scene of lazy canters under the palms has turned to work.

"This is definitely not as glamorous as it sounds: 'Spend your winter in West Palm Beach,' " said Michael.

It was, however, work rewarded for Henri Prudent and The King, Beezie and The Girl Next Door, Margie Goldstein and Saluut II, and

Chris Kappler and Suleiman. They won the four grand prix of the Winter Equestrian Festival and Florida. Each was played out on the spacious grand prix field of the Palm Beach Polo and Country Club's Equestrian Club.

For Beezie, the victory in the $30,000 American Bankers Grand Prix of Palm Beach was just one of many. Blue ribbons were in full bloom for Beezie and John Madden Sales. In all, she wound up winning eight classes in the month.

It very nearly was Michael instead of Kappler winning the final grand prix in February at the Palm Beach Polo and Country Club. He, Kappler and Jeffrey Welles were the only ones to make it to the jump-off out of a starting field of thirty-four. Welles went first, setting an intimidating pace but taking 8 faults, knocking down rails at the final fences, two oxers. Kappler was next, negotiating the course with the big, dark bay Suleiman clear in 31.17.

It was left to Michael and Heisman. The two took center stage of the scenic grand prix ring. One by one, they picked their way over the first six obstacles of the jump-off, five of which were oxers. At the final fences, with Kappler, a tall, sandy-haired, twenty-three-year-old Midwesterner watching, Heisman rapped the final rail, taking it down. He had the time, 30.24, picking it up as he made a sharp turn after the triple and toward the next to last fence. He also had second place because the final rail fell.

Riding into the warmup ring, Michael was greeted by Karen Golding, his barn manager, and D. D. "They know how to humble you in a hurry, don't they?" he said. Dismounting, he found Kappler, congratulated him and, after receiving his ribbon, settled into the comparative cool of the sponsor's tent and had a beer. It was the second time in two days that Michael had victory in hand, only to see it slide through his hands with a fault at the final fence. He and Vise were second in the $25,000 Winter Equestrian Festival Challenge Class, behind Enrique Sarasolo on Niratell.

It was in that same class that Kate got her first taste of big, really big, classes. Patty Harnois struggled to control her nerves as Kate and Ginsing prepared.

"This is the biggest course she's ever seen," she said, pacing the warmup area. "Ginsing is plenty of horse for it. If she can make it around here, she can go anywhere."

It was a big, long, technical course with a lot of jumps that greeted the pair. The section from the eighth through twelfth jumps was the one at which she'd have trouble. She was right. She finished with 16 faults, but with high spirits.

"Once I got riding I was okay," she said to Harnois, confident and "psyched" for next week.

But, in the end, February had proven to be frustrating for Kate. Sebastian, the ten-year-old, gray Dutch-bred stallion she had bought the year before as the horse to ride during her introduction to grand prix, had been hurt. At first it seemed as if it might be a slipped stifle. In the end, it appeared it was a strained muscle in the stallion's back. But the process of determining the problem was slow. Attempted remedies included massage and acupressure by Karen Pernell, and finally an internal blister, a series of injections of an iodine solution along his back and haunches by Dr. Steve Engle, a Florida veterinarian.

Too, there was rest. The return to competition would be slow. Margie would ride him in smaller classes, nurse him along. Allow him to heal and at the same time keep up his confidence. Kate hacked him, but when it was time to go in the show ring, it was Margie who was up.

*   *   *

After each day's show, Cobblestones was the place to be. The restaurant/bar in the Publix shopping center a couple miles from the showgrounds was the place to commiserate over bad rounds, toast the good ones and talk about showing horses. There were grumblings across the top of beer mugs that the Winter Equestrian Festival was too long, too big, too impersonal, too much like a factory and not enough fun. In this tavern owned by Dennis Witkowski, who once had played for the Washington Generals, the team foils that traveled with and consistently lost to the Harlem Globetrotters, the National Horse Show was another of the things that had people talking. There was a lot to say about the show.

By the end of the month, the National Horse Show had already started to tout the arrival of the show still nine months off. Programs to attract youth to the show were planned, including ones to allow Brownie and Girl Scout troops to earn their horsemanship merit badges. There would also be a petting zoo, pony rides and other attractions aimed at children. Pony classes would also return, a source of much complaint by riders.

And, around the small red tables, horse show people also talked about the retirement of a genius. In Europe it was announced that Jappeloup, Pierre Durand's well-known mount and 1988 Olympic and 1989 World Championship gold medalist, would retire at the end of the competitive year. The horse would make a farewell tour, ending its incredible career at the September horse show held at the foot of the Eiffel Tower in Paris.

CHAPTER 5

A New Way to Tampa Stadium

"Every year I drive up Dale Mabry Highway to the Stadium and I think to myself, 'This will be the year,' " said Michael about what may be one of the most important, and for him anyhow, the most elusive classes of the show-jumping year. "Afterwards, I drive back down Dale Mabry and I think to myself, 'Well, maybe next year will be the year.' "

Since its inception in 1973, the Michelob American Invitational's blue ribbon, its $30,000 first-place purse and truly its glory have evaded one of the greatest riders in the sport's history. Even when Jet Run, Michael's equine equal, was his mount, they were not the last horse and rider combination to walk back to center ring and receive the applause reserved for the winner. Michael has never tipped his hat as the crowd cheered his victory lap.

Like the Gold Cup at Devon, the show nearly in Michael's Pennsylvania backyard, the $100,000 American Invitational has escaped his considerable grasp. And that bothered him. Despite having had gold medals draped around his neck at the Pan American Games and the World Championship, and wearing the red coat and blue collar of America in a Summer Olympic Games, he has not won this class. He had won nearly fifty grand prix, but not this one held each spring in Tampa Stadium alongside Dale Mabry Highway's six lanes of concrete and convenience stores, used car lots and strip bars, a street named for a World War I flying hero who died in a freak dirigible accident.

In 1981 Michael and Jet Run were leading the jump-off with but four riders to follow. They finished fifth. Buddy Brown won that year on Felton.

That weighed on his mind a bit as the last days of the arduous Florida circuit unwound. He and Heisman had qualified for the class, winning $31,128 during the Florida stint to receive one of only thirty invitations. His girlfriend, D. D. Alexander, also saw her name and the name of her horse Bon Retour added to the list of what is considered one of a handful of premier classes staged in North America each year. Dina Santangelo, a young rider under the direction of Michael, was aiming toward the class but missed.

As the 1991 edition of this event approached, Michael had more to concern himself with than the fact that while he has the best record of any rider in this class, he has never won it. This year, one of the best horsemen in the world had to worry more about himself than about his horse or the course.

"Basically, the long circuit, the wear and tear, caught up with me a week too soon," Michael said, leaning forward and shifting for comfort as he sat in the concrete-walled tack room of the barn his horses occupied at the Florida State Fairgrounds, north of Tampa. "Timing is everything, isn't it?" and he laughed and shrugged.

The pounding that began ten weeks earlier had finally taken its toll in a class the Wednesday afternoon before. While showing Rhum IV in an intermediate class, the eight-year-old French-bred spooked. Michael was unsure of what caused it—a flag in the breeze, a woman with an umbrella—but the horse ran out at the last second instead of taking a fence. The quick, unexpected movement jammed Michael's back. The next morning, it took him twenty minutes to put on his shoes. His back was sore, stiff and spasmed.

For the next three days, it was a different Michael Matz for the run up to the Invitational. His purposeful, long-strided walk was shortened, and others from his barn exercised the horses. As he watched them school over fences or as students prepared for their classes, Michael hooked a heel over the lower rung of a fence at the working ring and leaned forward, stretching, trying to chase the kink from his back. At times he grimaced, the pain reminding him it exercised control over even as disciplined and dedicated a body as his. As he stood uneasily in a crisply starched blue oxford shirt and blue jeans, Michael watched D. D. conclude one of the most successful Florida campaigns of any rider. He also gained a deeper appreciation as Dina struggled with the perpetual back pain that had tortured her for more than a year. Dina's was so bad at Tampa that she had to be helped off her horse in tears after withdrawing from a class at the fairgrounds.

But not all of his recovery was left to stretching, standing and watching while others rode his horses. His lower back was too sore and the Invitational too big a class to try to work out the injury with simple exercise and a little over-the-counter pain relief.

Anheuser-Busch is one of the top corporate patrons of show jumping in America. August A. Busch, Jr., was an avid owner of horses, earning his way into the first group of people installed in the Show Jumping Hall of Fame at Busch Gardens, the amusement park in Tampa that advertises his family name. He introduced corporate involvement to the sport, buying the horse Circus Rose, renaming her Miss Budweiser and donating her to the USET. Arthur McCashin rode Miss Budweiser on the U.S. bronze medal team at the 1952 Helsinki games. Busch also owned several champion hunters, and rode with the Bridlespur, Missouri, hunt. Among the founders of the American Grand Prix Association, he put up the money to sponsor the first Invitational in 1973. That dedication to the sport was passed on within his family.

Elizabeth Busch Burke, daughter of the legendary St. Louis brewer, learned of Michael's injury. She arranged for him to see physicians employed by another Busch enterprise, baseball's St. Louis Cardinals of the National League. Taking spring training across Tampa Bay in St. Petersburg, the Cards opened their facilities to Michael at 6:00 A.M. for each of the three mornings before the Invitational.

Each day, Michael made the thirty-mile drive as the sun rose at his injured back. Once at the Cards' training room, he received ultrasound and deep heat treatments, as well as a massage to loosen the spasm. The ministrations of the Cards' trainer, Gene Dieselmann, and team physician Dr. Stan London were assisted by a prescription for Robaxin, a muscle relaxer. By Saturday afternoon, Michael was able to exercise Heisman and Bon Retour. While he was not well, Michael was at least well enough to take several jumps in practice. He did not enter any classes those last days at the fairgrounds, but he nonetheless could work out. Michael rode, though not with the élan that once prompted Charles Kauffman, owner of H. Kauffman & Sons, the historic Manhattan tack and polo shop, to compare him to ballet master Rudolf Nureyev.

Because, when you take away a rider's back, you take away much of his or her ability to communicate with the horse. A weak back also means weak legs, no leverage there, and it is the legs that signal and urge the horse on. Also, the back helps the rider stay balanced, and without an assured seat, a rider must ride with more caution than usual, anticipating trouble. Besides, there is the pain, a heavyweight's punch on landing after jumps or making turns.

After riding that Saturday afternoon, Michael slept, though not easily. On his bed at the Casa Grande Suite hotel on Princess Palm Avenue, Michael dreamed of being in a friend's private jet. Instead of a smooth, even, relaxing flight, the pilot was flying erratically. Michael woke startled and sweating, fearing for his life.

When he did dress and drive to Tampa Stadium, the site just two months earlier of the National Football League's Super Bowl, he made a change. Instead of driving up Dale Mabry Highway, Michael and D. D. drove her BMW up Buffalo Avenue. He was not being superstitious, just, well, cautious. Take your omens where you can. Besides, he already had one good sign—why not try for another?

On Thursday, after the day's showing was over, the riders qualified for the Invitational met in the sponsor's lounge at the State Fairgrounds. Michael walked stiffly into the meeting, holding D. D.'s hand in one of his and an O'Doul's nonalcoholic beer, brewed of course by Anheuser-Busch, in the other.

After a pep talk from Gene Mische, creator of the Invitational, the order in which they would ride was drawn. First drawn were the names of the riders. Then they drew numbers for their starting position. Michael's name had been drawn first, but when his order of go was matched to it, he was thirtieth, the very last rider. Not only did this give him the advantage of seeing every other rider negotiate the course, but more importantly gave his back time to rest. The possible downside was the weather; after twenty-nine other horses had ridden over it, even the well-drained course at Tampa Stadium might be mired and miserable. After all, it had been the rainiest March on record, and this, the last weekend of the month, was not to be the exception.

It rained off and on during most of Saturday. It was, however, clear at the Stadium at 5:00 P.M. when the gates were opened so riders and trainers could walk the course.

The first time around the 660-yard, seventeen-obstacle course designed by Steve Stephens, Michael walked alone, concentrating, measuring strides to each jump, touching the top rails to judge how stable they were in their cups. As to be suspected in a class as large as this, Michael found some resting on flat metal cups, platforms really. Even the slightest rub would send such fences crashing.

While Billy Joel music caromed off the gray cement walls of the still-empty stadium, various Anheuser-Busch products flashed across the Sony JumboTron screen perched at the south end of the stadium. D. D. walked the course on her own. So did the other riders who filtered in, walking among the technicians preparing to videotape the event for broadcast a week later on ESPN, the perpetual-sports cable channel.

Also walking the course were other veteran riders. Many had yet to add their names to the list of winners of the Invitational, a show that also serves to keep riders in Florida until the end of the circuit. Hap Hansen meandered through the jumps with Philip Cillis, assistant trainer with Hansen and rider of Juniperus. Other riders who have won numerous other classes but not the Invitational talked among themselves and others. Barney Ward. Debbie Shaffner. Anne Kursinski. Ian Millar, the Canadian who most in the sport consider among its top stars. George Morris, though not riding that night, walked the course.

Only one of the riders walking amid the jumps, most of which doubled as billboards for everything from a local grocery chain to the ubiquitous Anheuser-Busch products and Johnny Walker Black Label Scotch, had won this event three times. Her appearance at 1991's Invitational was no less an accomplishment. But those were secondary to the fact that she was even alive to ride in it.

Katie Monahan Prudent, the current first lady of American show jumping, walked the course, preparing to ride Silver Skates that night only because of the narrowest of victories. With just a week left in which to qualify and her best horses sidelined with injuries, the thirty-seven-year-old rider from Middleburg, Virginia, had finished fourth in the Volvo Grand Prix at the fairgrounds the previous Sunday, winning $4,000 and making an invitation a long shot but nonetheless a possibility. Then, just a bit more than forty-eight hours before the start of the Invitational, she and Silver Skates won another $6,500 in another class, qualifying them for the Invitational.

After she rode out of the grand prix arena that Thursday, Monahan Prudent was engulfed in the congratulatory handshakes and kisses of just about every rider, trainer and groom milling around the in-gate. They had ached for her to qualify. They wanted to see her ride in the Invitational, it seemed, more than she did.

Monahan Prudent entered the final week of competition with no intention of even trying for the Invitational, a class she had won on

Noren in 1983, on The Governor in 1985 and on Special Envoy in 1988. Her two main mounts this year were injured. Make My Day, a thirteen-year-old Thoroughbred had pulled a back muscle. Nordic Venture, a ten-year-old Oldenburg, strained a suspensory, the ligament that supports the ankle joint, in the cursedly deep sand of Wellington. And Special Envoy, the thirteen-year-old Hanoverian she had ridden to Horse of the Year honors in 1988 had been sold, Pamela (Mrs. W. Averell) Harriman shipping it to new owners in Italy.

It was left to her and Silver Skates, a horse she was still getting to know, to propel her once again into Tampa Stadium for the Invitational. It did, and afterward she hugged and kissed husband Henri and son Adam, as well as Bert and Diana Firestone, owners of the ten-year-old gray mare that had quickly earned the trust of Monahan Prudent.

That Thursday Katie Monahan Prudent was living a different life from the one she had just a year earlier.

March 2, 1990, Monahan Prudent was riding in a Friday qualifying class before the Cadillac U.S. Open Grand Prix at the Palm Beach Polo and Country Club. It was just a bit more than two months after Adam, her first child, had been born. At the third element of a triple combination, Special Envoy stumbled. The twelve-year-old Hanoverian gelding swam through the fence and Monahan Prudent fell. She walked from the arena on her own, but once in the warmup area collapsed. She was flown by helicopter to the Wellington Regional Medical Center. After four hours of surgery, a blood clot was removed from her brain.

There were dozens of people in the halls of the hospital as she recovered, and many more greeting her as she left—albeit with a doctor's caution she might never compete again—a week later. Just twenty days after her near-fatal fall, Monahan Prudent rode a horse. About two months later she was the leading rider at the Children's Services Show in Farmington, Connecticut. In June, less than a hundred days after she had nearly died, Monahan Prudent was fifth in the jump-off at the grand prix of the Upperville, Virginia, Colt and Horse Show. Still, the 1990 season had been difficult: a new child and recovery from as serious an injury any rider has had and lived to tell about made the already-demanding season test her.

Walking the course as spectators trickled into Tampa Stadium a little more than a year after she lay in a hospital bed, her riding future, if not her life, up for grabs, Katie's smile was as wide as the biggest oxer on the course. She laughed with other riders, and compared notes with her husband, who would also ride in the Invitational that night. She even had time to snuggle with Adam. That night, there was nothing for her to lose. There were no assumptions. She could afford to ride free on the new gray mare and let happen what would. That she was even there seemed victory enough.

As Katie and Henri Prudent strolled among the jumps, a wave of people emerged from the in-gate at the northeast corner of the stadium. At the lead was the crown prince of the sport, and with him its royal family, at least of the commercial side of show jumping in this country.

Greg Best walked into Tampa Stadium that Saturday night in late March in black dress loafers rather than knee-high riding boots. He wore a blue blazer and not a hunt coat, tan slacks instead of white riding britches. If Monahan Prudent had surprised the sport's competitive clan by being one of just thirty riders to make it to the Invitational, then Best had stunned it by not being invited. The Olympic silver medalist, fourth-place finisher in the previous year's World Championship, the rider of the best jumping horse in America, if not the world, was a spectator that night.

Gem Twist didn't even arrive in Florida until late. Most assumed that with the number of shows between then and the Invitational, Best and the horse former rider and CBS television commentator Robert Ridland, once compared to the National Basketball Association's Michael Jordan, would make it. They had in the past, winning the event in 1989, and making it to the jump-off in 1990, the year Best's buddy David Raposa and his own big gray horse, Seven Wonder, surprised the crowd by winning.

America's most recognizable horse and rider combination were not riding in America's biggest show. Best and Gem Twist hadn't won enough money during the Winter Equestrian Festival. He was two riders below the thirty being invited. With Andre Dignelli ahead of him, it would mean two riders would have to decline invitations in order for them to ride. That didn't happen.

So, that night, the sport's biggest in this country, its best horse did not leave his stall and his rider played tour guide.

Someone asked publicist Marty Bauman who Best was ushering around and he said, "That's Mr. Busch. Not the president, the important Mr. Busch."

Best strolled into Tampa Stadium with August Busch III and his family. He walked from jump to jump with an entourage, explaining the vagaries of the course, how riders would attempt to conquer it and how the horses might feel about riding under the lights with 15,000 people cheering. He smiled in unison with the Busch family in front of the most curious jump on the course, a vertical that was the second half of a combination. Holding up the rails of this particular obstacle were two large fiberglass killer whales, orcas modeled after Shamu, the star attraction at Sea World, yet another Anheuser-Busch tourist attraction, this one in Orlando.

Best, like most of the other riders still walking the course, signed autographs for the fans who would fill less than 20 percent of the stadium's 74,296 seats. The Invitational opened the gates to allow spectators to stand next to fences as tall as they were, to let their eyes bulge as they considered the tight triple combination Stephens had set along the east side of the stadium. As mostly young girls approached to secure the signature of the man who rides Gem Twist, Best's smile and polite demeanor masked the feeling of anticlimax that gripped him.

On Friday, as the final junior jumper classes wore on at the Tampa Fairgrounds, Best slouched near the grand prix ring in a golf cart and watched. For a moment Best was joined by John Madden, a man as gregarious as Best, at least at the time, was subdued. In play, Madden grabbed Best's arm and twisted it.

"Go ahead," Best deadpanned. "Couldn't make it any worse."

Later that same day, Best attended the riders' meeting for the Invitational. Before it ended, he ambled out of the pre-Invitational meeting alone and into the late afternoon sun, which cut a shadow across his face under the visor of the cap. That shadow lengthened as Best showed a tight smile, shrugged his shoulders to a man at a nearby phone booth and lowered his head to walk away. Two days later, the morning of the American Invitational, Best sat at a picnic table near the concession stand and played backgammon with friends.

Saturday night, though, he was in the stands of Tampa Stadium to watch as thirty horse and rider combinations made a parade lap around the stadium and Lisa Burke, an ESPN commentator and hunter rider, sang the National Anthem. He watched a class that lived up to Bauman's pre-show publicity.

James Young, a thirty-year-old from Zimbabwe, was the first rider to tackle the course its designer called "straightforward and without a lot of tricks." Aboard Wait & See, Young had a rail at the second jump, and clipped the first half of the Shamu combination. Young then aimed toward the number 5 fence, a vertical sponsored by Publix Markets and dressed up as a produce stand. At the last second, Wait & See decided to do exactly as its name suggested, and instead of jumping, sent Young cascading into the fence.

It was an intimidating start for the night.

Barney Ward, the forty-six-year-old former semiprofessional football player from Bedford, New York, and his horse Annaconda did little to change that outlook. They, too, had the second fence down, as well as 9B, the second half of the combination. When the twelve-year-old gray Westphalian mare refused at the third part of the combination, Ward withdrew.

Then came Susie Schroer and Charlebois. They luxuriated in a round of applause as they cleared the last effort, a 13½-foot-wide water jump, and broke the timing beam with the first clear round of the night. Lisa Jacquin and For The Moment did the same after Cillis and Juniperus had a surprising 23 faults. It was becoming difficult to tell how the course would jump.

Chris Kappler and Suleiman had 11 faults, and Christian Currey on Fox Cattle Company's Mirador were clear with the exception of a rail at the second fence. Garant, Enrique Sarasola's Hanoverian, was undone by both ends of the number 4 combination, the fence that would eventually bedevil many riders.

Next to ride was Margie Goldstein, a Miami native who rides nearly every class as if it were her last. She walked into the stadium on Saluut II, a Dutch-bred gray horse as competitive as his rider. Goldstein started the course as if she intended to give herself a birthday present a day early. She cleared the triple rail to begin, flew the numbers 2 and 3 verticals and had no problem with the Shamu combination. Goldstein and the 16.2-hand gray stallion attacked the rest of the course ferociously, spurred on by a loud cheer as she negotiated the tight number 9 triple combination.

After clearing the number 13 vertical, Goldstein found a bit extra in Saluut II, and they galloped hard toward the final obstacle, the water jump flanked with a wild array of flowers. They launched from the far side, landed smartly on the near and were about to post the third, and most impressive, clear round of the night. Mere feet from the timers, Saluut II made an uncontrollable veer to the right and cut off course. They missed the timers, collecting 3 faults. They had to circle back through the timing beam to complete the round. The audible sorrow of the crowd chased the echoes of its earlier cheers from the stadium.

Seven of the night's remaining eight clear rounds followed: Eric Has-brouck on La Juste Valeur; Tim Grubb, who screamed to get his horse

Ever through the triple combination; Leslie Burr Lenehan on Pressurized, who kicked out a middle rail of a fence but was clear because it didn't lower the height of the fence; George Lindemann, Jr., on Threes & Sevens, the Quarter Horse who was clearly a crowd favorite; Jeffrey Welles on Serengeti; Tony Font and Lego; and Michael Dorman on Olisco.

But Michael Matz had watched as D. D., just four rides before his own effort, became one of eight riders to have 4 faults on the evening. Bon Retour, the Argentinian-bred chestnut gelding she and her mother own, clipped a rail on the number 12 oxer, excluding them from the jump-off.

Neither did Katie Monahan Prudent make it to the jump-off. She was wildly welcomed as she rode into the ring, and her appreciation for the crowd response was visible on her face as she circled the course in preparation to jump. Excitement built as she cleared jump after jump, but was deflated as she had a rail down on jump 9C, the last element in Stephens's demanding triple combination. Still, there was some sort of victory for her as she rode off, the applause as loud as when she had ridden in.

And Beezie Patton was not among those in the jump-off. She and Northern Magic had down the first half of the Shamu combination and the first part of the triple.

As with Best watching from the stands, there was anticlimax in the ride. Madden and Patton together had brought the ten-year-old Dutch-bred to a fine edge in the week before the Invitational. They had qualified easily, winning $29,200, so were not scrambling to win money, the basis of all but ten of the thirty invitations issued. Two nights earlier, a portly full moon suspended over Tampa, Madden coached Beezie as she jumped Northern Magic under the lights of a small ring at the Fairgrounds. While jumper and dressage riders traded places in a $25,000 novelty team class, Madden and barn manager Terry Bradner set a course in one of the sand warmup rings. As they had other nights that week, Beezie and Northern Magic practiced so the horse could become accustomed to—maybe even bored with—performing outdoors under the lights.

Beezie rode Northern Magic nearly flawlessly over the training course as the horse's owners, Frank and Marilyn Fisher of Milford, Michigan, watched. It was as if they were attending an outdoor concert on a warm summer's evening, watching a virtuoso perform with a casualness borne on the night air. It was a strong performance, one that pleased Madden and Beezie, the horse less spooky with each ride. The next night, Beezie rode Northern Magic under the lights, but did not jump, saving its strength for the Invitational Saturday night.

Then, Saturday night under the lights of Tampa Stadium, Northern Magic was undone by that which had menaced him in other classes in Florida. As he had earlier, the ten-year-old Dutch-bred had trouble with the combinations. He knocked down the first part of the Shamu combination and the initial element of the triple, a wall with a little liverpool in front of it. Beezie shared some of the blame for the first fault, getting a little too close to the fence for the best possible takeoff. At the triple, Northern Magic was a little too aggressive for his own good.

Riding into a combination, horses have more to see, more to distract their attention. When this happens, they often look beyond the first element, and it becomes a surprise as they close to it. That is what Northern Magic did at the triple.

"All week we worked on combinations because the only faults he had in the two grand prix in Tampa were in the triple," said Beezie. "He was in a rut, he had become nervous about the combinations, so jumping in he was a little bit aggressive. But other than that, we were real pleased with him. The lights didn't bother him. He felt very brave and confident."

The big chestnut's problem with combinations was nothing new. Beezie and John had seen it before, and it was something to be worked on, polished. In the past, with Beezie and John working on the problem, combinations became, with added effort, all but free jumps for Northern Magic.

The night's last clear, as it should have been, was posted by Michael. There were no visible signs of a sore back as he and Heisman, a thirteen-year-old Oldenburg, ambled into the stadium. Announcer Peter Doubleday, in his scholarly introduction, had not mentioned Michael was riding with an injured back, with pain as a handicap.

"I just hope I can do my horse justice," Michael had said earlier in the day. Heisman, in fine form, got from his rider as good as he gave during the final ride of the first round of the Invitational. Heisman rattled a rail at the third to the last fence, the green oxer that D. D. and Bon Retour had knocked down, but otherwise was clear.

Waiting for the jump-off, Michael wanted to sit and rest but was afraid his back would stiffen. While the three newest inductees into the Show Jumping Hall of Fame—Kathy Kusner, the late Arthur McCashin and United States Equestrian Team mount San Lucas—were honored, Michael paced. He pressed his hands on the small of his back and bent forward as organizers of the Invitational honored the military effort in the Persian Gulf, the war orchestrated by Tampa native General H. Norman Schwarzkopf. He put the heel of his boot on a stack of wood pallets in the chute under the stadium and stretched long as he had for the last three days. And he walked.

"One down. One to go," Michael said, walking to the stabling area to check on Heisman. As he hoped they would, instincts built on almost twenty-five years of riding took over, beating back the pain, getting him to the jump-off. He hoped those deep-grained habits, layer upon layer of doing the right thing day after day in schooling rings and during competition, would sustain him for another thirty seconds or so.

He would find out shortly.

The seven-effort jump-off course ready, Schroer stepped Charlebois to the gate as her trainer and owner of the horse, Paul Valliere, offered his final instructions: "Don't look back, kid." She didn't. Schroer piloted the sixteen-year-old Thoroughbred gelding over the numbers 7, 8 and 13 fences, the Shamu combination and the numbers 11 and 12 jumps to post a clear jump-off round in 34.366 seconds.

"I can't ask for any more than that," enthused Valliere as he stepped down from the grandstand to greet Schroer as she rode out.

As she had in the first round, Jacquin followed Schroer's clear round with one of her own. She rode For The Moment to a clear in 33.986 seconds, allowing her to enjoy the lead.

Hasbrouck and La Juste Valeur had 8 faults. Grubb and Ever had 4.

Lenehan and Pressurized were next. The 17.1-hand, rangy Thoroughbred used every bit of his sizable stride to blaze the course, prompting one of the in-gate hangers-on to remark, "They're taking no prisoners tonight."

They did, however, take 4 faults. Their 32.317 seconds stood as the fastest of the night on the jump-off. It was to no avail. They crashed the Shamu vertical, eventually finishing fifth.

The crowed roared its approval when Lindemann and Threes & Sevens walked into the Stadium for their go at the jump-off. The noise owed some of its volume to the new-found patriotism that had overcome most Americans since the Persian Gulf War. Threes & Sevens, a Quarter Horse, was one of six American-bred horses in the ten-horse jump-off. Clearly he was an outsider in a sport long dominated by hot, leggy Thoroughbreds and the more placid, big-boned European Warmbloods.

Lindemann called on some of the barrel-racing agility in the Quarter

Horse's blood, and the speed from the racing side of the breed that night. They were clear in 32.916. The four remaining riders had to stay clear but go faster still.

Welles and Serengeti were neither. They had 8 faults in 35.85 seconds.

Font and Lego entered the stadium with an excellent chance to catch Lindemann. Font rode the course hard and masterfully, and looked to have found the secret to saving time. After the number 11 Budweiser plank fence, every other rider to this point circled left around the number 6 jump for a straight shot at the final fence, the Johnny Walker spread number 10. After Lego cleared number 11, Font cut the horse hard left, ducking below the number 6 fence and relied on Lego's surefootedness to make it over the final fence clear.

They were clean and fast, but not fast enough. Font had pushed Lego to a clean 33.670 seconds, even with the shortcut. Lindemann, standing at the edge of the stadium wall, broke into a smile, his eyes wide in disbelief behind his horn-rimmed glasses.

Dorman and Olisco followed, but posted 7 faults.

The last ride of the year's biggest class was left to Michael and Heisman. George Morris leaned over the edge of the grandstand to offer some course tips to Michael as he walked Heisman through the chute and into the glare of the Stadium lights. He started slowly, coaxing increasing speed from the horse Matz had called "a gentleman, a joy to ride." But the horse owned by Sale Johnson, of New York City, had a rail at number 8 and, like Lenehan, had the second half of the Shamu combination down. Eight faults.

Michael, wearing a Neoprene back brace borrowed earlier in the day from Illinois dressage riders Betsy and Uwe Steiner, walked the horse out of the ring, congratulating Lindemann as he did. Near the stabling area under the grandstands, Michael gingerly dismounted and handed Heisman over to Doug Lahr, the horse's groom.

America's most successful active show jumper was quiet for a few moments, watching the toes of his highly-polished black boots as he walked. Leaning against a huge supporting beam, standing in the sad half-light under the grandstand, Michael said, "I had trouble in the jump-off on all of the circuit. What is it about this class?"

D. D. stood near. Then smiling she said, "He didn't give you any extra."

Michael smiled, tilted his head to one side and shrugged.

"He's a heartbreaker. Heisman's a heartbreaker," she said, then locked her arm through one of Michael's, and they leaned on each other smiling.

Michael was eighth that night, collecting $2,000. Lindemann won it and $30,000. Font was second. They were followed by Jacquin and Schroer, the only others to have double clear rounds that night.

While Lindemann gave interviews with ESPN and the print media gathered in the press box 150 feet above the course, Michael and D. D. compared class notes with other riders. They talked with Ian Millar, the former stockbroker who had had 8 faults on Czar, the horse he was riding as Big Ben, Canada's answer to Gem Twist, recovered from its second colic surgery in about a year. They stood with Katie and Henri Prudent, cheery and congratulatory, like couples saying good night after a Christmas party. Michael smiled as he signed autographs, and watched as grooms tended to Heisman.

"Hey, that's show jumping," he said, and walked off to check on Heisman. Afterward he and D. D. drove back down Buffalo Avenue to his hotel room, thinking that while the new route didn't change his luck, it was, at least, a shorter drive.

Unlike many of his colleagues, Michael was not flying to Gothenburg, Sweden. He and Heisman were among the Americans to qualify for the Volvo World Cup Finals to be held in April. Ten years earlier he and Jet Run had won the event when it was staged in Birmingham, England. While Heisman could easily finish in the top ten, even in the small indoor arena, he chose to bypass the trip to Sweden.

With a Quarter Horse beating the European Warmbloods in the American Invitational, Katie Monahan Prudent an unexpected entry and Greg Best and Gem Twist not even competing, the Florida circuit for 1991 came to an end. The month had literally roared in on lion-like winds that canceled the last grand prix of Wellington, and floated out on the giddy euphoria that usually accompanies exhaustion.

Michael did not win a grand prix during Florida. He finished second in two, third in one and had a trunkful of sixth-, seventh- and eighth-place ribbons. As much as Michael believes in being consistent, always getting a piece of the prize money, the lack of a grand prix win in Florida gave him slight pause.

Beezie practically owned the speed classes here, winning eleven of eighteen. She also won a grand prix in Wellington. It was easily her best Florida trip to date, one which had extra meaning as she saw Northern Magic begin to regain his successful form of the previous year.

Kate had to wait to make her debut in a grand prix. Bad weather had turned the footing at Gainesville slippery, and her planned first grand prix at the smaller HITS show was passed by in favor of a trip to Texas's spring string of shows. Still, it had been an instructive and successful Florida.

Elsewhere in the Sunshine State Lt. John O'Brien of the Florida Department of Agriculture and Consumer Services continued to untangle the web surrounding the death of Streetwise.

And the Tampa portion of the Florida circuit was not without a pall of its own. Horses had died here, but for reasons vastly different from those which claimed Streetwise.

On March 23 Mario Deslauriers was riding P.D.Q., a black Selle Français, in a Gambler's Choice class under the lights at the fairgrounds. In the sponsor's lounge adjacent to the ring, there was mock gambling and a $100-a-plate dinner to raise money for the Show Jumping Hall of Fame. It was a festive evening, and a light counterpoint to a circuit that was grinding to a close.

Deslauriers and P.D.Q. appeared headed for a victory that night, their first of the Florida season. After the last obstacle, the fourteen-year-old horse apparently twisted its right front ankle. It hobbled after passing through the timing beam, and the festive air drained from the evening like helium from a leaking party balloon.

Dr. Tim Cordes said P.D.Q. had broken P-1, the first pastern bone. It was a sagittal fracture, one that breaks from the front of the bone straight through to the back and, in P.D.Q.'s case, ran the length of this bone located below the ankle and similar to the bone between the first and second knuckle of the human hand.

"It was a horrible, horrible fracture," Cordes said, his face contorted at the thought of the pain that had shot through P.D.Q.

The prognosis was not good. The healing process would be even more painful than the break itself. It would mean at least six months of stall confinement, bone rubbing on bone until the joint fused, leaving the horse peg-legged if it recovered at all.

Deslauriers, with the consultation of several veterinarians, made the toughest decision a horseman ever has to make. The twenty-six-year-old Canadian living in Culpeper, Virginia, gave his approval to Cordes injecting the horse in the neck with a concentrated barbiturate solution, humanely destroying the animal. It was a horse he had bought for himself only a couple of months earlier at the beginning of the Florida circuit, a horse for which Deslauriers had high hopes.

"You can never have enough euthanasia solution," said Cordes, who at Tampa also had to put down a horse suffering colic. "But, thank God, at least there is something we can do."

*   *   *

Just south of Tampa, in Sarasota's Doctors Hospital, physicians ran out of things to do for William Joshua Barney, Jr. He died of emphysema.

Josh Barney, to many, was the National Horse Show for many years. After prep school at Choate and graduation from Yale in 1933, he joined his father's construction company and entered the equestrian community through his marriage to Priscilla Payne Harvey, who rode hunters and jumpers.

Though never a competitor himself, Barney was a national and international judge. More importantly, Josh Barney became a patron of and then officer in the National Horse Show and the United States Equestrian Team. He eventually served as secretary, president and chairman of the National Horse Show. He and his wife lent horses to the USET, including Master William, Hugh Wiley's mount when he won the George V Cup in London and when he finished seventh in the 1960 Rome Olympics. And Barney served as treasurer of the American Horse Shows Association, which honored him just months before his death at the age of seventy-nine.

Josh Barney's passing was the second of its kind in a handful of months for the American show-jumping community. The summer before, while Americans competed in the World Championships in Stockholm, Patrick Butler died.

Like Barney, Butler was a patron of the USET, sending it some of its greatest mounts. Among them were Balbuco, grand prix riding's top horse in 1976 and the AGA's Horse of the Year in 1979 and 1980. He also owned such horses as Untouchable, Old English, In My Cap, Mystic and Sloopy, the latter being Neal Shapiro's mount when he won the bronze medal at the violence-marred 1972 Munich Olympics. He also was part owner of Touch Of Class, which Joe Fargis rode to the individual and team gold at the 1984 Los Angeles Olympics. Butler also was part owner of Mill Pearl, another jumper Fargis rode to greatness.

For this and his other works, Patrick Butler was among the first group of people and horses named to the Show Jumping Hall of Fame.

He was eighty-nine when he died.

Beezie Patton and The Girl Next Door during a class at the Tampa Fairgrounds in March of 1991.

Grooms and horses await their riders before a class at the Winter Equestrian Festival in Wellington, Florida, 1991.

Michael Matz and Ginger at the Winter Equestrian Festival in Wellington, Florida, 1991.

Kate Chope and Vitales at the Pin Oak Charity Horse Show in Katy, Texas. It was her first grand prix.

Michael Matz and Herald Square at the 1991 Devon Horse Show and Country Fair.

Leslie Burr Lenehan.

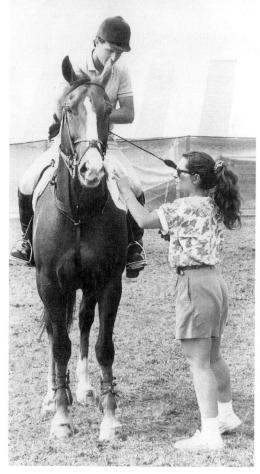

Alice Debaney, rider of The Natural.

Texan Tony Font and
Lego with Font's
girlfriend, Tanya Lemons.

David Raposa and Seven
Wonder.

Groom Francisco Ventura gives a bath to
Hector during the Winter Equestrian Festival in
Wellington, Florida, in January 1991.

Debbie Dolan.

Kate Chope plants a kiss on the nose of
Ginsing.

Ginsing, left, and Hearsay, right, await their turns in an amateur class.

Kate Chope and Hearsay during the Crown Royal Motor City Grand Prix at the Bloomfield Open Hunt near Detroit.

John Madden, right, and Beezie Patton with an entourage of amateurs walk the course before a class at the Crown Royal Motor City Grand Prix near Detroit.

Beezie Patton and John Madden examine a jump before the Crown Royal Motor City Grand Prix.

Michael Matz in the warmup area before a class.

Anne Kursinski.

Barney Ward chats with Kate Chope and groom Tammy McHugh before a class.

Tim Grubb, Chris Kappler and David Raposa before a class.

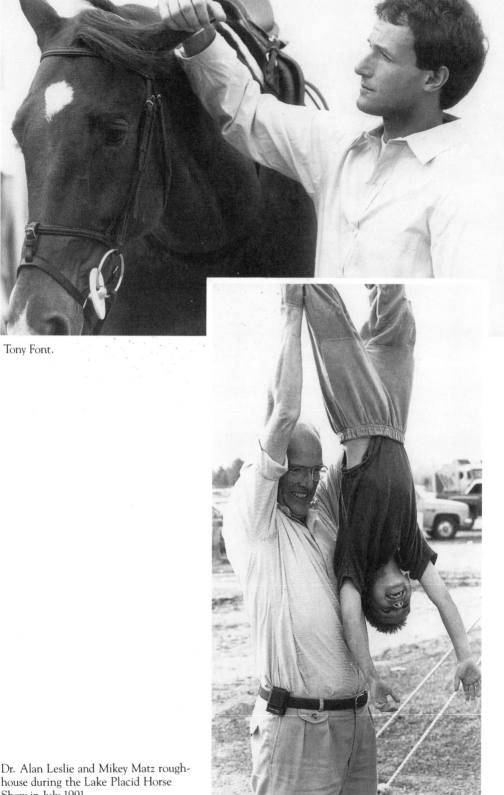

Tony Font.

Dr. Alan Leslie and Mikey Matz rough-
house during the Lake Placid Horse
Show in July 1991.

CHAPTER 6

A Good Place to Start

Travelers on Interstate 75 shared the road with horse vans and trailers in among the vacationers seeking the sun on Easter vacation. So did I-4 north to Orlando and Daytona Beach. There also was plenty of traffic from Tampa Stadium back to Wellington, a week or two of rest before the long ride to home pastures.

The show-jumping road show was breaking camp, sending its many members in various directions for different purposes. For some, it was a time to recharge, rest themselves and their horses. They headed north for the gentle springs of Virginia and Maryland, and the questionable ones of Pennsylvania, New Jersey, Illinois and New York. For others, the arrival of April meant the southern migration of the winter would simply be replaced with the westerly one of spring. More and more riders headed west to the growing spring season of Texas and, to a more limited degree, Oklahoma. And there was the golden allure of California. For the lucky few like Greg Best, Hawaii, its golf courses, and some clinics and a horse show to judge beckoned.

Still others flew east, to Sweden and the Volvo World Cup Finals in Gothenburg. A handful of Americans competed in the international event held April 11–14 and sponsored by Volvo. Two placed in the top ten finishers.

Debbie Shaffner on Volan and Anne Kursinski on Starman tied for seventh place. The next highest finisher was Candice Schlom on Wula, tied for twelfth with Jan Tops of Holland. Jeffrey Welles and Serengeti were sixteenth, Donald Cheska and Bailey eighteenth, and Susan Hutchison on Samsung Woodstock and Michael Endicott on Mon Bambi were tied for twenty-second.

Most considered America's showing somewhat less than inspiring, and another indication that the mighty Americans had slipped from their lofty perch atop international show jumping. John Whitaker and Henderson Milton, Britain's Gem Twist, won the championship for the second consecutive year.

Several other Americans—Chris Kappler, Todd Minikus, and Debbie Dolan—did well in other classes, but no championship came home with the Americans. Kursinski was, however, voted the Leading Lady Rider.

Beezie and John headed home. There was work to do in Cazenovia, at the Moons' farm in Port Jervis and, especially for John, in Europe. Beezie and Terry took turns driving Beezie's car home. John flew to Europe. It would turn into a marathon trip, one of prospecting for horses in several countries, places that in the past had proven to be more productive than the polo fields of south Florida had been this winter.

On Easter Sunday, Michael flew from Tampa to Philadelphia. As he was doing that, his children were flying from Montreal to Philadelphia. They would meet at the airport and then drive back to his Vintage Farm in Collegeville. Michael would rest his back and his horses, catch up with his racing Thoroughbreds and enjoy being Michelle and Mikey's father, the activity he most enjoyed.

Like Michael, Kate headed home, driving to Tallahassee and then flying north to spend time with her mother on Cape Cod. It was a short visit, one intended to tie up the loose ends of applying to veterinary school, but also a time to eat at a kitchen table and not a restaurant booth, to take clothes from a closet, not a piece of luggage. Kate also took time to catch up with friends, something important to her.

Then, she returned to the road.

Kate flew from Boston to Tallahassee to pick up her car. Then she headed out alone. Driving west on I-10 through Alabama, Mississippi, Louisiana and Texas, she was on her way to her postponed grand prix debut in Houston. This was the territory of singer-songwriter Jimmy Buffett: Spanish Fort, Pascagoula, Biloxi, Baton Rouge, Beaumont and eventually Houston. However, Kate didn't have the likes of Buffett's "Cheeseburger in Paradise" or "Margaritaville" drawling from the tape player of her BMW. Instead, she was serenaded by Paul Simon, Squeeze, Joan Armatrading and, for mood purposes, Michelle Schocked's "Memories of East Texas."

As she drove she had time to miss Tammy. When the Florida circuit closed, instead of heading back to Holly Hill on Cape Cod, Tammy signed on with Ronnie Beard, a round-faced trainer whose Wyndmont Farm is located in Jamison, Pennsylvania. She had spent nine years at Holly Hill, a veritable lifetime for grooms in the show world.

It was a time to catch up with a college friend. From the cellular phone her mother had given her at Christmas for just such road trips, Kate called a friend in Birmingham.

She also had time to think about Florida. It had gone quickly, too quickly. But it had been a critical time, one during which she had focused on her riding just as she set out to do. Kate was pleased with the results. She had ridden often, getting to know Ginsing and keeping her confidence up with Hearsay, reliable as ever. Now, cutting across the bottom of the country, she knew that it was now time to dig in and prepare for the summer, the bigger classes, the massive travel schedule. "This is the year to do it," she told herself as she drove. She knew she was living the realization of a dream, one that had begun years earlier.

On the first day of her trip, Kate made it as far as Baton Rouge. On the first trip across the Deep South, Kate was hoping to do some sightseeing. None got done, she had too many miles and too little time.

The next day, still not believing that the Florida circuit could already be over, Kate arrived in Katy, Texas, about thirty miles northwest of downtown Houston. The skyline of Houston rises like one of the space vehicles monitored at the nearby Johnson Space Center. But in Katy, off-season home of Boston Red Sox pitcher and *enfant terrible* Roger Clemens, Houston is an image in a commuter's rear-view mirror. Out here, Texas's most cosmopolitan—disturbingly so for West Texans—of cities gives way to the suburban sprawl and the post-modern–pre-oil-patch-bust offices of oil companies along the Katy Freeway, the highway that shoots west eventually to Austin.

Mason Road off the freeway was the perfect example of how Houstonians have, like residents of other big American cities, left center city behind, subdividing the flat lands that used to be farms. From where it humps over the freeway and heads south, Mason Road is a sampler of American business. It is a collection of stores, franchised fast food restaurants, strip centers and garden supply stores. It is a block deep, this commercial conglomeration. Behind it are housing developments.

For a stretch of about two miles, Mason Road heads south in its exhibition of free marketeering in overdrive. Then, abruptly, as if interest or money suddenly dried up, this intense business district ends. Instead of stores lining the divided highway, there is grass, knee high as if the lawnmower had run out of gas just as the oil patch economy, Houston's raison d'etre, did.

About another mile further Cinco Ranch, a development of $100,000 to $400,000 houses, erupts from the flat land. Nearby is the Great Southwest Equestrian Center. Up a quarter-mile-long driveway is a mansion, the center of this facility built when oil and money flowed. Behind it are stables, a polo field, permanent stalls and several indoor warmup rings, and the main arena. It is not as architecturally correct as the Brendan Byrne Arena of the Meadowlands, and the stalls are not nearly as nice as the ones at the Palm Beach Polo and Country Club, but it is a suitable show facility. Still, the "Great" in Great Southwest Equestrian Center seems a bit of Texas hyperbole.

This was home for, among other activities, the forty-seventh annual Pin Oak Charity Horse Show, a gathering of some five hundred horses, including Shaky Tails—saddlebreds and walking horses—as well as hunters and jumpers. This was the fourth year Pin Oak had been at the Great Southwest Equestrian Center, having moved, like many of Houston's residents, to the suburbs.

Walter Bloxsom, a fourth-generation Houstonian and independent oil and gas geologist whose daughter Charlotte would win the AHSA Medal class at the show, was president of the show that started its life at the Pin Oak Stables on Post Oak Boulevard. Like Paul Greenwood at the National, his mission had been to save the Pin Oak, a charity horse show that had donated some $3 million over the years. His first move was literally that, a move from May to April, avoiding the hideous heat and humidity that gives residents a new appreciation for air conditioning. Still he had to do more, so the show added classes other than hunters and jumpers. The 1990 version of the show opened with more than five hundred horses entered, an increase over previous years, and renewed enthusiasm.

But as the National had left center city for the suburbs, Bloxsom saw Pin Oak's long-term salvation as a return inside the "loop," the highway that surrounds Houston proper.

"Pin Oak rakes up a lot of memories for a lot of people, but a lot of them no longer come because it is too far away," said Bloxsom. He was hoping to have Pin Oak back nearer its roots by year's end.

On a show morning when rain fell in sheets thick as Bloxsom's Texas accent, he was in a golf cart. In the back and on the seat next to him were large white boxes. As grooms and riders got about the business of preparing for the day, Bloxsom, president of the show, drove the main aisle connecting the stabling areas.

"It's the donut man," he'd say.

Then he'd stop, grab a box, open it and offer donuts to anyone who happened to be around. It was a small expense and a small gesture, but a gesture nonetheless, welcome to many exhibitors who often feel as though they are there for one reason in the eyes of show managers: to write checks. It was something not seen at many other, much larger shows. If such goodies were dispensed at all, they were handed out by underlings, by hired hands, not the president of the entire show, not the person in charge.

"Don't worry, it's not really raining," he'd say. "This is just Houston humidity."

That was just one of the differences evident as horsemen in Texas gathered for a show. This was an easier-going show, one without some of the competitive electricity crackling in the air of those in Florida or in the East. For sure, it was a grand prix event, just one with a little less pretense, a little less nervousness. That is the nature of show jumping in Texas.

"People like Joe Fargis and Debbie Shaffner have come here, tried it and liked what they found," said Charles McDaniel, a tall, slim Texan who learned to ride at the age of five or six when he was at a party and fell off a horse, sustaining the laughter of girls also at the party. "It's not necessarily easier, just different, and we don't have as many good riders as they do. But those who can are just as good as those in the East. Face it, there are a lot of bullets in the East. Sure, some of them look down their noses at us, but nobody here takes it personally."

Besides, there's less stress. "Hey, who wants to go to a show and have to school horses at two or three in the morning?" said McDaniel.

Rusty Holzer agreed. The New York City rider who wears the colors of the Virgin Islands was making his first trip to Texas. He was enjoying it.

"The atmosphere here is far more relaxed," said Holzer. "It's not so cutthroat as it is in the East. People here actually help you. Some people in the East have lost sight of the fact that this is supposed to be fun."

Tony Font was a little more to the point: "It's not just the East and only the East any longer. There are a lot of nice horses here. Candice [Schlom], Suzie [Hutchison], Bernie [Traurig] and Hap [Hansen] are on the West Coast, and all have good horses. It's hard to find anyone who could outride Hap, but he didn't make it to the World Championships because he was from the West Coast and the rule-makers are from the East."

If there was an embodiment of the difference between show jumping in the East and in Texas, it was Orley Dehoyos. The fifty-two-year-old Mexican-American had ridden and trained hunter-jumpers in Texas since he was ten years old. In that time he started riders like McDaniel, William Martin, Riley Robertson and Alan Smith, all Texans, all successful.

"Sure, the East looks down on us," he said. "But they're snobs, and to them we're all cowboys. Folks from the West don't see it that way. They're nice. Hell, Texans get along with anybody."

One of those riders who found the Great Southwest Equestrian Center an accepting place, one in which to stretch, was Vicky Miller, not a typical rider at this level. She was sixteen and riding full time in the big amateur classes and the grand prix of the Midwest and Southwest. She had made her grand prix debut here two years before.

At sixteen, Miller rides as a professional, not as a rich kid dabbling with horses. She does it full time. She does well. The year before she had $70,000 in winnings.

Miller grew up in Kent, thirty miles south of London, England. There, where children rode jumper ponies instead of hunters, she was more interested in horses than going to school. Because of that, her parents gave her a choice: school or horses, do one and do it well. She never made it to a prom or even a history class after that. The family moved to the U.S. in 1988. Geoffrey Miller, her father, leased construction equipment in England, but felt about golf the way his daughter felt about horses. It was while watching the Master's tournament on television that he decided that Augusta, Georgia, was the place to live, so he sold the business and moved his family to nearby Atlanta. Since then, the family traveled the horse-show circuit of the Midwest and South, living out of a thirty-eight-foot camper—Miller, her parents, and three younger sisters.

The 1991 stop at the Pin Oak Horse Show was proving to be a good one for Miller, the prodigy daughter of the former Linda Bradley, who had show jumped in England. She had won the Conoco Caper, Pin Oak's version of a Gambler's Choice. Early in the week she had also placed fourth and fifth in an open jumper stake. The show was going well as

Miller approached the Paolo Gucci Show Jumping Hall of Fame Series Classic for junior amateur owners.

The class began with Christian Currey and Fox Cattle Company's Oliver going second and clear. Clears were posted by Belynda Bond and Miller. Kevin Coleman, who shows with and drives truck for Goldstein, was best by a round with 32 faults on Ashjoff. Kate went next on Vitales, the mountain of Dutch-bred on which she posted 8 faults. Six rides later, it looked as though Kate would join the handful of clears. Ginsing was going well, and Kate riding confidently. In the end, they pulled a rail at the fifth jump, and ended with 4 faults.

Then it was Miller's turn again. Riding Betty Boob, the talented woman/girl seemed about to prove why it had been the right choice to drop out of high school and begin riding as a professional.

Miller had a winning round going until the combination, 4A and 4B. She cleared the vertical well enough, but at the oxer, one that was plenty wide, Betty Boob lost speed and Miller lost balance. The pair crashed into the oxer, Miller pitching forward and onto the ground in front of the mare.

Miller lay helpless on the floor of the Great Southwest Equestrian Center arena as the horse came down heavily, first the front left hoof and then the rear one on the same side on her head. Both blows slammed into her temple. Miraculously, even after the impact of the crash and the hard fall, Miller's hunt cap stayed on her head, so when the horse walked across it, there was some protection. This was a plain hunt cap, no extra padding, no chin strap, nothing but luck to keep it on and little more than that protecting her head.

The arena was quiet as she lay there among the rubble that once had been the oxer she crashed. Dennis Mitchell, her trainer, was the first to reach her. Other riders, grooms and eventually an emergency medical technician made it to the arena. Miller was more stunned than hurt. She stood just as someone arrived with a stretcher, and in tears was helped to one of the show offices for treatment.

The next day Miller walked a little gingerly, moved a little slower. She joked with fellow riders that she felt like Mickey Mouse, brushing back her hair to show sizable lumps on each temple. Still, she was a Mickey Mouse that was alive, when just as easily she could have been the reason for a moment of silence before the grand prix.

Miller, like the majority of grand prix riders, wore only a light, velvet-covered hunt cap in the ring. Michael and Beezie wore similar headgear. So did Best, Lenehan, Morris, Jeffrey Welles, Fargis and Goldstein.

Barney Ward wore a battered hunt cap, while his son McLain wore one with clear plastic straps securing it to his head. Anne Kursinski wore and appeared in ads for a helmet with a leather harness. Currey wore a similar headgear. So did Kappler and Hansen. Kate was among those mostly young riders who wear helmets with harnesses when they ride. She said it was the only condition her mother put on her when she began riding jumpers. Katie Monahan Prudent, even after a life-threatening head injury, wore the traditional hunt cap, no harness.

With the possible exception of the criteria used to select members of the USET, helmet regulations was the topic most likely to cause a ruckus among riders. The AHSA had wrestled mightily with the issue, revising guidelines, postponing them, putting them into effect and rescinding them. Horse magazines carried lengthy articles on the topic. There was much discussion not only on how safe the new helmets were, but how they looked as well. All that occurred even after a Centers for Disease Control report that listed horseback riding more dangerous than riding motorcycles or racing automobiles, with some 17,500 head and neck injuries occurring during the two-year study period.

Vicky Miller, sixteen, riding as a professional in a sport considered more dangerous than racing in the Indianapolis 500, had only a small layer of fiberglass and a smidgen of velvet between her young skull and the hooves of a horse when she fell at the Pin Oak. She also had a lot of luck.

*   *   *

The next day Kate stood in front of the grand prix course posted on a bulletin board near the in-gate. She was crisp in a white blouse, a monogrammed collar snug around her throat, helmet on, and a deep blue jacket. A finger traced the grand prix course she'd soon be riding, the first grand prix course for her. Certainly it wasn't the biggest set of jumps she had ever seen. Some of the amateur classes in Florida and the WEF Challenge Series were bigger. But they had been outdoors, set on the mammoth grand prix of the Palm Beach Polo and Country Club with plenty of room to gallop and consider. This was in the much cozier confines of an indoor facility, tightening it, closing in on the horses.

It was not raining as the grand prix began. It was not pouring. It was not a deluge or downpour or driving. It was not constant or steady or heavy. It was all of that and more. Horsemen with stalls at the outer rim of the stabling areas built dikes. Horseshow classes routinely perform in the rain, but several in the Pin Oak outdoor annex ring were canceled.

Kate, at first cognizant that this was to be her first attempt at a grand prix, was a little nervous. That faded after she was able to school her horses in the grand prix ring that morning, giving them a good look at the place. It didn't return as she walked the course with Margie, striding between jumps that were at least as high as her chin. It was then that the storm outside turned Wagnerian, pelting the metal roof of the Great Southwest Equestrian Center and punctuating the intense tapping with shattering cracks of lightning and thunder.

Goldstein had six horses going in the class. Kate had two, Vitales and Ginsing, both long-strided horses for whom the course shouldn't be overly imposing. Besides, Kate had two good draws, going eleventh and twenty-fifth, so there would be plenty of time to watch others go, and sort out the trouble spots. But with six mounts Goldstein would need help getting horses limber, a job for Kate, so her otherwise slow, almost peaceful round would be made hectic.

She watched, this time as an owner, as Goldstein put Sebastian through a clear round. Miller, sore but game, looked as though there had been no brush with death just the day before and rode Pilot Point boldly, in the style of her hero, Goldstein. It seemed as if she'd be clear until she clipped the third part of the combination and crashed the round-closing Cadillac jump, one that bedeviled many riders in the grand prix.

With her mother in the stands, Kate rode into the arena of the Great Southwest Equestrian Center on Vitales and onto her first grand prix course. The day before had been the first time she had ridden Vitales since he had shipped in from where he was staying in California. Before her, Goldstein had made the course look manageable. Others had struggled, many with the Cadillac jump, which was set at an odd angle to the one before it. She entered the ring with a grin on her face, not one of cockiness or one set there to mask fear. Instead, Kate seemed truly happy about the opportunity to ride the big course for the big money. The weather did too. The thunder was silenced. No lightning flashed. Even the rain let up.

Her chances of a clear round ended at the second fence. Four faults. Then, she and Vitales seemed to organize and set their collective selves on finishing with no further knock-downs. However, the combination undid that; 10A for 8 faults, 10C for 12. Then, like many of the horses that afternoon, Vitales tried to make kindling out of the Cadillac fence. Sixteen faults.

Still, when she rode out of the in-gate, she repeated the broad smile she had on the way in. She walked past Goldstein on Lincoln, who was on deck, following Tracey Feeney and Infinity, who turned in one of the surprising clears of the afternoon.

Fourteen rides later, Kate and Ginsing entered the ring, passing Rusty Holzer and Aroganz, who had just gone clear.

Again, smiling, Kate started her ride. Again, she struck the second jump, but this time it stayed in place. The big gray rattled the fourth fence, and it too stayed in its cups. Then at the next fence, 5A of the combination, there were 4 faults. She also had down the Johnny Walker planks, which were perched on flat cups. Again, 10C came down, and the damnable blue and white Cadillac planks at the end came down. Sixteen faults. Again. And again she passed Goldstein on her way out, this time as she rode in on Daydream, normally her puissance horse.

The course, in the end, also claimed McDaniel, and Miller, and Font and his trusted Lego, the hometown favorites. The jump-off had five horses returning, three of them ridden by Goldstein.

Sebastian went first, taking 4 faults at the Johnny Walker planks, the jump that had helped undo his stablemate, Ginsing. Then came Feeney and Infinity: clear in 37.921. The young woman from Dallas lit up the ring with her smile afterward. It was only her sixth time in the ring with the horse, and his first crack at a grand prix course. Next was Goldstein on Lincoln, a horse owned by Frances Snodgrass, a local woman who adored both the horse and its rider. They were clear, and .019 faster than Feeney and Infinity. Holzer, a senior at Harvard University, was clear on Aroganz, clear and deliberate at 39.559. Finally, Goldstein was back in the ring with Saluut II. They cleared the eight-effort jump-off course clean and in a winning 37.475, to finish first. She also was second and fifth.

Then the rain stopped and the sun came out.

"All three stallions pulled through," said Goldstein after. She then pronounced Saluut II as an Olympic-caliber horse. "Sebastian went very, very nice, but he was just a little too fresh, he wasn't taking it seriously. He can be Peck's Bad Boy when he wants to be."

She was even more pleased with the performance of Sebastian's owner.

"I'm very pleased with the way Kate rode," Goldstein said. "That was a tough combination, especially for a long-strided horse. That was a very difficult last fence, but Kate gave both horses good rides."

Kate too was pleased. Ginsing had gone better than he had during the week. He got a little nervous at the triple and shot forward, which made the last fence difficult. Vitales had gone well, considering she hadn't even hacked him before tapping him to be her first ride in her first grand prix.

Still, it had gone well. She felt confident. She understood what the troubles had been. It was tempting to stay on in Texas instead of going to California as planned. She liked the nature of the shows, the pace, the feeling.

"Here, if you think you can do it, they say go ahead and try," said Kate. "In the East, there's pressure to do it well if you're going to do it."

In the end, she'd head to California, the first trip there for either her or Goldstein, and see how different Bakersfield and Del Mar could be from the East. There'd be five shows in five weeks there before a return to the Houston National.

If nothing else, California would be drier than Houston. At day's end, four inches of rain had fallen on the area, causing flash floods. However, Kate's California trip was cut short when she dislocated her shoulder. There was no fall, no crash, no drama. She popped it out coming out of the ring after a class, and had to fly home to recuperate.

CHAPTER 7

The Main Thing on the Main Line

Greg Best stood near the southwest corner of the arena, looking over the hats of women lining the waist-high rail. The day's heat had crested at 98 degrees with smothering humidity, yet there was no trace of discomfort as he stood, a bemused smile under his aged hunt cap, his white knit tie knotted tightly and hunt coat over a long-sleeved shirt.

His brown eyes narrowing in thought, he looked over the grand prix course still being built and said, "Sixteen years. I haven't done anything for sixteen years, except come to Devon."

For a bit less than two-thirds of his twenty-seven years, Best had spent the last part of each May at the Devon Horse Show and Country Fair. He won the lead line class here when he was three years old.

He shook his head as he wandered off to ride in that night's grand prix, the centerpiece of what may be America's most traditional—and successful—outdoor horse show. While he has never won the grand prix here, this horse show for Philadelphia's Main Line harbored nothing but the best of memories. Like every other rider, Best said Devon was special, different, a refreshing stop on the year-long treadmill of shows, a good way to start the push through the swelter of late spring and summer toward fall's indoor season.

Winning at Devon is different from winning anyplace else. Even placing well here is better than winning at other shows.

Part of that has to do with history; few shows have been around for ninety-five years. The Devon Horse Show began while Grover Cleveland was in the White House and the Supreme Court's Plessy v. Ferguson upheld the notion of separate but equal. It started not as the society event it became and remains, but as a utilitarian gathering. The Devon show began as a way of encouraging farmers in the Delaware Valley to produce more and better carriage horses. If that were the need today, we'd have a government-subsidized program instead.

This quest for better carriage horses itself was a response to a move made earlier by the Pennsylvania Railroad, which, to increase its passenger service revenues, encouraged Philadelphians to live in a community other than the one in which they worked. Suburbs blossomed in the Gay Nineties, and when captains of industry arrived home by train, carriages awaited. There was, as a result, always a need for horses. Besides, the well-to-do hunted more and played more polo now that they were off the streets of Philadelphia and in the countryside.

From there, the ladies and gentlemen of the Main Line helped it prosper and grow. From the first show in 1896 with 100 horses entered in 29 classes, Devon's horse show grew. The ninety-fifth anniversary show in the late spring of 1991 attracted 1,600 entries in 30 divisions and over 400 classes.

And, as usual, it attracted hundreds of volunteers. The Devon Horse Show and Country Fair is the closest thing to a common religion in this part of Pennsylvania geographically north of Philadelphia and socially superior to most every place else. Instead of being a product, the Devon show is a process. It begins shortly after the dust has settled following the last class in the main ring and continues with increasing fervor until it opens with a weekend strictly for young competitors.

All those volunteers are needed—some to staff the food booths, including one that proffers broiled lobster tail, while the idea of haute cuisine at most other shows is to put Grey Poupon on the hot dogs. Others sell a staple of Devon: lemon sticks, a long, slender piece of lemon-flavored hard candy poked into a partially cored lemon. The eater of this treat sucks the lemon juice through the candy straw and then eats the candy. Volunteers are also needed to make the more than 3,000 pounds of Devon Fudge sold during the show. John, a self-proclaimed expert on such matters, sang the praises of this sweet, but added hastily that it was not the only reason he came to this, his favorite show of the season.

"I love Devon," he said. "I think it's great. Without question it is my favorite show of the spring, and one of my favorite shows of the entire year. It's too bad there aren't more like it. It has very nice stabling, very nice facilities, always good footing and always good prize money. People act like they like to have you here. If I have a nice horse, I want him to win at Devon. Devon is important because it is Devon."

Volunteers also operate the concession, which, as much as any one thing, helps give Devon its special appeal. The old Tea Room has since been taken over as a commercial booth, but tea is still served to show-goers. In its earlier days, the Tea Room was called the Beauty Shop, volunteers being treated to steam baths as they brewed tea. Even in this day of corn dogs and mesquite-grilled chicken, the ladies of the Tea House at the Devon Horse Show and Country Fair serve tea sandwiches, the offending crusts trimmed away.

There is a reason for all of this industry, all of this tradition. As successful as it is as a horse show, Devon is equally successful as a benefactor for the Bryn Mawr Hospital. Since 1931, the show has raised $6.645 million for the hospital.

"I've been to every horse show in the United States, every major one, and most in Europe, and I know of no other show that makes as much for its charity," said Richard McDevitt, the retired trial lawyer who was president of the Devon Horse Show. "Recession? I haven't noticed any recession. As a matter of fact we have more sponsors this year than we've ever had before."

Like many other things at Devon, the grand prix is different. Instead of being staged on Saturday night or Sunday afternoon, it is held on Thursday evening. More tradition.

Oppressive heat—the high nineties—clung to the showgrounds when the $50,000 Michelob Grand Prix of Devon approached. Some smaller classes were concluding in the hunter rings as the water truck pulled into the Dixon Oval, the main ring at Devon. Just as the driver opened the spigot and began to spread water over the dusty surface, it started to rain. For ten minutes it poured, thunder growling in the distance.

About two hours later, the in-gate under the metal sign proclaiming "Where Champions Meet" swung open so riders could enter and survey the course Frank Chapot had set for the evening under the lights. As the start drew near, all of the riders filtered out. All, that is, save one: George

Lindemann, Jr. He stood near the center of the ring alone, almost as if he were communing with the jumps. He finally left.

With a light rain beginning to fall, Best rode into the Dixon Oval just as he had so many times before. He rode out with 12 faults. The Devon grand prix was under way.

Beezie and French Rapture were next to go. Despite the fact that he forecast no problems with the footing—a near-perfect mixture created by Harry Gill, the recipe for which was guarded more closely than the one for Devon Fudge—John had screwed small studs into the front shoes of the thirteen-year-old Dutch Warmblood. They proved helpful, but seemed at first to not be enough. Beezie and French Rapture had ¼ time fault. Then, after Stacy Casio and Boss & Company—all of his horses are named after the American shotgun manufacturers—went, the time was adjusted, as is allowed, and Beezie and French Rapture were clear.

After that, it became a night of clear rounds. A lot of clear rounds. Fully fourteen of the thirty-three entries made it to the jump-off, which went off in front of 3,500 spectators.

As the first round unfolded, it rained harder. Then it rained harder. Then harder still.

It was a certifiable downpour as Michael and Heisman were greeted with a hometown roar as they rode into the oval named for the man who for years had kept this rider so well mounted. Then, Michael's Devon jinx took over and the pair had the first fence down. After that they were fast and clear.

"It was his first show back," said Michael. "He went in looking around at the crowd. He didn't have his mind on his business." Besides, some of the stallion came out of Heisman. This was breeding season, and while he was not servicing mares, Heisman had a natural distraction. "I'm not making excuses for him. He jumped the hard part.

"I wish there was a home field advantage. Devon is close to home for me, so the crowd might be a little bit on our side, but as many times as I've disappointed them, I'm surprised they even clap anymore."

Best, by now soaked with a mixture of sweat and spring rain, and Gem Twist entered for their turn. They too left with 4 faults.

The first five riders in the jump-off all had trouble with the course. With that many in the jump-off, everyone had to be fast, there was too much room for a change in the standings. Beezie and French Rapture had 8 faults. Henri Prudent became the fastest 4-faulter. Kappler's first trip was toughest in the jump-off; he and Suleiman collected 32 faults.

Lindemann's stay in the ring after walking the course may have helped in the first round, but in the jump-off he and Threes & Sevens, his trusty Quarter Horse, had 4 faults . . . the last rail. Michael Dorman and Olisco had 12.

It wasn't until Lisa Jacquin and For The Moment went that the Devon faithful had a clear jump-off round to cheer. The pair enjoyed leading the field for two rides. Concorde, the fourteen-year-old Hanoverian-Thoroughbred cross on which Kappler had won the $35,000 Children's Services Grand Prix earlier in the month, had 4 faults. Lindemann returned on Abound and had 16.

Leslie Lenehan and Fortus opted to move up in the jump-off order. And for a while it paid off. They were clear, and their time of 36.18 was enough to give them the lead.

"I always feel like a lost little kid on him," Lenehan said to owner Jane Forbes Clark as she rode out of the ring. Then, dismounted, she grabbed Clark and said, "Where were you standing when I went? Let's get back there, it's lucky."

Not lucky enough.

Anne Kursinski and Starman returned for their shot at the jump-off. Their aim was true as they mastered the course clear and fast, moving in front of Lenehan and Fortus by 1.5 seconds and Jacquin and For The Moment's time by about 2.5 seconds. For at least one ride, it looked as though Kursinski might win at Devon the way she had at the $60,000 Pepsico Empire State Grand Prix at Old Salem Farm earlier in the month.

Then it was Debbie Dolan's first of two shots at Devon's jump-off. She and Arrangeur made the most of it. They picked their way through the course, shaving a little more than half a second off Kursinski's time, moving into first.

She rode off to the applause of her trainer Conrad Homfeld, who was standing in mud that oozed over the top of his boat shoes. She made a quick change, getting off Arrangeur and onto her other jump-off horse, V.I.P.

While she warmed up, P.S. Gazpacho and Diane Shaw navigated the course, picking up 4 faults.

Alice Debany and The Natural were ready for their attempt at the jump-off of Devon. Debany was sure The Natural was ready to be great, ready to be on at the same time she was. The first four jumps were proof of that; clear and on the time of Dolan and Arrangeur. Then she made the tight right turn to the next jump, pleased because this maneuver had been a problem for her in the past. But she then failed to move up quickly enough to get the seven to a pair of very forward oxers.

"I don't know what happened," said Debany afterward. "Maybe I landed and waited a moment, congratulating myself or what, but there was a mental lapse that was all my fault. By the time I moved up, seven was no longer a reality, so therefore I started packing in eight, but eight was a little too dead and slow as well for the two. I kicked with all my might to get out, and he tried to get out with all his might. We didn't make it and we had the back rail."

But what made the jump-off memorable for Debany was what happened as she was trying to kick out. She was working so hard that she somehow flipped the reins around her neck.

"My instinct was to try to salvage it," she said. "I'm facing a five-foot plank, but hey, I'm still on my feet, there were a lot of four-faulters in the jump-off. I put him deep, maybe he wouldn't need a lot of release, and I was wrong. When you have the reins around your neck, they're kind of tight. He got no release, and as hard as he tried, his hind end didn't make it.

"A lot of riders probably wouldn't see the humor in that, I suppose. It was either circle and wimp out or go for it, and I did. Both he and I tried when we got in trouble."

Out of the ring, she was laughing at her bit of unintended acrobatic riding. She apologized to her horse and then replayed her plight with dressage rider Robert Dover, who was at the in-gate.

Then it was Dolan's second shot at the jump-off. While they went clear, it wasn't imperative to be fast. They finished in 37.20, fourth behind Lenehan. After, she again quickly dismounted, hugging Homfeld in the process. This time she was getting back on Arrangeur for the victory lap.

While some filtered off to dry out and get wet at the Clydesdale Corner, the bar under one set of grandstands, an improbable pair of riders headed to Devon's press box to meet reporters. One was Dolan, the winner. The other was Kursinski, the runner-up. The season before, these were the two riders at the center of the USET selection lawsuit. Dolan had been on the Team for the World Championships, only to be replaced by Kursinski. Now, they were facing the press at the same time, something not lost on that same group of reporters.

The inevitable question arose, something about the irony of her beating Kursinski after Kursinski replaced her on the Team. It was something about enjoying that feeling, a question that danced around the edge of the unasked: "Revenge is sweet, isn't it?"

Dolan, a small woman with a smile like the new moon, wanted to talk about her horses, Arrangeur first and V.I.P. fourth, but said, "I say hello to everyone every day at the horse show, and I always will, no matter what is said or what is written about me." With reporters persisting, the pain and problems of the Stockholm excursion were replayed.

The youngest of six children, Dolan was "the tag-along little sister" when her two older sisters began riding. "It just went from there," she said. Dolan rode at several barns on Long Island near her home. Eventually, she showed junior hunters and equitation with Ralph Caristo, progressing to the Medal and Maclay competitions until she graduated from Old Westbury's School of the Holy Child and went to Fairfield University, where she double-majored in finance and economics ("I loved what I studied, though I've never done anything with it"), and rode with Leslie Burr Lenehan at Fairfield Hunt.

"He made it fun," said Dolan. "It was a real neat barn, nice people, fun kids. All of my memories of riding with Ralph are great. Going to horse shows was fun."

In 1982 Dolan's involvement with horses deepened when she purchased Albany from Jimmy Kahn in California. She rode the 17-hand Thoroughbred in the amateur classes, and Lenehan showed the big gelding in the open classes. In 1983 and 1984, Lenehan rode Albany to AGA Horse of the Year honors, and placed him on the gold medal Olympic team at the 1984 Games in Los Angeles.

"He was a very special horse," said Dolan, who had retired him earlier in the year. "He had tons of personality, and he loved to jump. An incredible trier. If he possibly could, he'd jump the jump and jump it clean, he never didn't try."

It was on Albany that Dolan won her first grand prix. It was 1986 in Cleveland, where Dolan's relatives live.

"There must have been thirty-five people there for me," she said. "And it seemed like he knew. It was like he really wanted to be good there."

Albany and Country, a jumper who won just about every amateur championship around, came to Sagamore Farm in 1986. Combined, they spoiled Dolan for any horse to come.

"Those were my first two jumpers. I thought they all were supposed to be like that. They gave me confidence. They made it fun."

Along the way, she purchased V.I.P., a Dutch-bred black stallion who had been ridden by Steve Stephens before being added to Dolan's string. Unlike Albany and Country, V.I.P. did not inspire love at first sight for Dolan. The first time she rode him, he ran away with her.

"He was very different. I had had all Thoroughbreds and he was a

Warmblood. It took a long time, but when it finally began to work, it really worked. If it was a big course, I wouldn't want to jump it with any other horse than that one. There isn't anything you can build that he can't jump. No matter what I get him into, he gets me out."

But it was Arrangeur that had won it for Dolan that rainy night in Devon. It was the kind of weather that Dolan hated, the kind in which she doesn't always ride her best. Still, she rode. She won. Devon that night was about as far from the controversy, as far from the lawsuit, as far from the acrimony as the Main Line is from Luxembourg, where she found out that it would be Kursinski and not her on the team.

That she won was a certain testament to what had gone on in the past year.

"It was a lesson in life," Dolan said. "Last year was extremely difficult for me. It took a lot to keep going. There were a lot of nights when I cried myself to sleep, but I had the support of my family and my friends and they pulled me through it. Now I just go in and do the best I can. This year is this year, and I want to have fun. Tonight was fun. I can't say last year was very fun.

"I got slaughtered by the press. I wasn't given a chance. They ripped me apart and I can still come back. I believe in what I did. I stuck by it and I pressed on.

"I made the USET change to a better system so that it was fair to every rider, so it doesn't matter who you ride with, or how much money you have or don't have or what political connections you have. If you're good enough, you'll go."

Still, it was difficult. Dolan did not enjoy a lot of support within the community of riders. She was blamed for everything from filing a costly and unnecessary lawsuit to single-handedly making it impossible for American teams to ever win again in major international competitions.

In the face of that, Dolan continued. Why?

"I love my horses. I love to ride. And I love to win."

When the unease of the press conference dissipated and the questions ended, Dolan smiled a thank-you. Still dripping, still spattered with mud, she tucked the winner's cooler under her arm and walked into the night, back to where Arrangeur and V.I.P. waited in their stalls.

*   *   *

Ironically, it was about this time that the USET announced it was joining the computer age. They were doing it with the assistance of IBM. Big Blue had agreed to sponsor the Team's computer ranking of horse-rider combinations, the listing that would be used to select teams for international competition. It was about as popular as Dolan's lawsuit. Just about everyone had a complaint about it, including Tony Font, who suggested it was just another way for the eastern equestrian establishment to control the sport. Others thought it was suitable as a guideline, but that the final decision should be left not to a computer but to a trained eye, someone familiar with the sport.

But time marched on at the USET.

*   *   *

In the end, Michael once again could not find the combination to win at Devon. Still, it was better than the year before.

"In 1990 I fell off For A Moment and Caribe," said Michael. "I was on the ground more than I was on the horse. I was about ready to take the gas pipe."

But Devon was not necessarily easier for Michael and the rest of Vintage Farm. It's close to home, so instead of being less work, it's more. There were horses to ride and other work to do at home before coming to the show.

Still, the place had memories for him. He had ridden here twenty years ago in the local classes, appearing on horses owned by J. Basil Ward. Early in his career, Michael had also ridden Mighty Ruler at Devon, winning the stake class once in the early 1970s.

Work was far from done even after Thursday night's grand prix. D. D. and Dina had Pan Am selection trials to ride in. D. D. and Bon Retour were perfect, a fault-free round. Dina and Manassas County were the same.

*   *   *

Important as it was, as brimming with tradition as it was, not everyone made it to Devon. Kate and Goldstein were still out west. Back in Texas, Sebastian, the back injury of Florida all gone and fully regaining his old form, won the $32,500 Crown Royal Grand Prix in Irving, Texas.

"It was a weird feeling," said Kate. "I was the owner accepting congratulations for the horse, not the way I rode. It was a little like being a parent, I would guess."

Also at Irving, Vicky Miller, the sixteen-year-old who had cheated death at the Pin Oak Charity Horse Show a month before, finished ninth on Pilot Point.

CHAPTER 8

The Challenge of the Rain

Robert Dobes and José Santa María of the Garden State Fireworks Company stood in the humid air on the first night of summer and watched trails of smoke drift away. Moments before, the last of their handiwork had climbed skyward and burst, filling the sky with great slashes of light. Below, John Somers conducted the six members of the Garden State Brass Ensemble—wilting in tuxedos—into "Stars and Stripes Forever," a bit early, trying to keep up with the hummers and whistlers, crew jets, peonies, reports, and chrysanthemums that lit up the night skies over Gladstone, New Jersey.

Then, as the last echoes of the fireworks were absorbed by the nearby pine woods, the rock-jazz-pop band Best Kept Secret added another layer of patriotic frosting on the cake of the evening, whipping into a medley of Elvis songs. The band had many of the four hundred or so people attending the USET's Star Spangled Gala dancing until late Friday night became early Saturday morning. The mansion at Hamilton Farm is sheltered with trees, ones that kept the music from escaping into the neighborhood. No music reached the headquarters of Beneficial Finance (owners of the former Brady farm), or the home office of a group of small weekly newspapers that had been collected like Fabergé eggs by the late Malcolm Forbes.

Randy Leoni, a blur of energy in a short white sequined dress had orchestrated the gala, the first of its kind to be held on the back lawn of the turn-of-the-century country estate of James Cox Brady, a New York City financier whose farm once covered 5,000 acres in three northern New Jersey counties. Her chin-length brown hair bobbed in time to the music as she strolled along the periphery of the mammoth tent that had been set up below the terraced formal gardens leading down from the mansion. She smiled a lot, fielding the kudos rightfully lobbed to her by USET members, patrons, competitors, employees and friends who had supped on poached salmon and tenderloin of beef. It was a fine party, no better way to begin summer, no better way to mark a unique ten-day series of competitions.

In the middle of the festivities, while Best Kept Secret rested its horns, William Steinkraus took the stage. He thanked those attending and apologized for the fact that the Johnny Walker products had been locked too safely away to be on the four bars when the party began. This five-time Olympian also introduced USET Gold. This was not an equestrian award, but a designer perfume. Two friends of the USET who wished to remain anonymous had donated the research and development of this perfume, a mixture of scents including—not surprisingly, since it was aimed at an equestrian crowd—the smell of new-mown hay. Each woman at the gala received a sample. The $125 per half-ounce bottle would help underwrite Team activities for years to come.

The Star Spangled Gala was part of the Festival of Champions staged by the USET for a variety of reasons. Not the least of these was to elevate its profile and kick off the drive toward the 1992 Summer Olympics. As major celebrations and competitions go, this was not one with an extensive history of plotting and planning. The idea had been hatched only five months before, a brief time for pulling together major dressage, show jumping and driving competitions, not to mention a world-class garden party.

The thought was to concentrate several major competitions in one place. Hamilton Farm, the boyhood home of Treasury Secretary Nicholas Brady and for the past thirty years the headquarters of the USET, seemed the likely spot. After all, it was the Team that would select dressage and show-jumping riders to represent the U.S. in the Pan American Games and designate the whips who would drive in the upcoming World Pairs Championships. The USET also selects a dressage and show-jumping champion, so why not combine all of these events in a ten-day stew at

USET headquarters, spice it up with an interdisciplinary competition and hope that it gets the public's interest piqued and its checkbooks opened.

Moreover, the Festival of Champions, held June 13–22, would be a perfect run-up for a similar bash during the upcoming Olympic year. In that respect, the first Festival of Champions may well have been the most successful dress rehearsal ever. It certainly was one of the most elaborate equestrian events of the year.

In addition to the dressage and show-jumping championships and final Pan American selections, the Festival also was an attempt to imbue young riders with the feeling, the sense of history of the place. There were clinics with top riders and competitions designed to keep the supply of young blood flowing into the veins of the USET.

Beyond that, the Festival was supposed to be fun. It was supposed to create some goodwill. The centerpiece of that effort was the Challenge of Champions, a good-natured attempt at cross-pollination of the three disciplines. Four teams consisting of one show jumper, one dressage rider and a driver competed, the catch being they participated in the two events other than their own. The drivers jumped and performed a third-level dressage test. Dressage riders drove and jumped, and the show jumpers drove and showed their skills in the dressage ring.

Despite the fact that some of America's top equestrian athletes were performing in their national championships, it was the Challenge of Champions that drew the most attention. Rightfully so. It was, in a sense, like that granddaddy of all non-sports sports programs, "The Superstars," in which athletes from various sports went head to head in events other than their own.

Michael teamed up with dressage rider Linda Smith and driver Sem Groenewoud. Greg Best's New Jersey Knights team was rounded out by dressage rider Heidi Erickson and Tucker Johnson, a long-haired, ever-smiling driver from nearby Oldwicke. Debbie Shaffner was one of the Blonde Bombers, along with dressage rider Betsy Steiner and whip Sharon Chesson. The final team linked George Lindemann, Jr., with Olympic dressage rider Robert Dover and noted pairs driver Larry Poulin. They prophetically called themselves The Ultimate Winners.

Had he the temperament for it, Best could probably do well as a dressage rider. That is, if he could overcome the nasty habit of going off course, which he did as he rode in the large sand ring behind the Team's headquarters in what was once Brady's horse barn. Lindemann, for a show jumper, is fairly well polished in the dressage ring, and Shaffner thoroughly enjoyed the change of horses and events. Michael looked natural, at ease, on the back of the bulky Warmblood on which he performed his dressage test, wearing his hunt cap instead of the more formal top hat. In the end, Poulin, whose cousin Michael is an expert dressage rider, won the dressage phase of the USET's equivalent of "The Circus of the Stars."

It was in the driving that the abandon and competitiveness of the show jumpers began to show. This was the last of the three events, and the prelude to the grand prix on the final day of the Festival.

"If I could drive and do the dressage as well as they jump, we'd be okay," said Best before he took the reins.

With Johnson at his side, Best drove Johnson's powerful pair of grays. Shaffner, with boyfriend course designer Steve Stephens supplying humorous commentary to the crowd gathered near one of the obstacles on the course, finished her driving at the gallop. Michael was studied and serious driving Groenewoud's pair. Lindemann won the driving portion of the event, ending it by nearly running Kennebec Count and Kennebec Russell, the matched Morgans Poulin drove in the 1985 World Pairs Championship, into the woods as he exited the obstacle course. Poulin grabbed the reins to assist and avert any trouble.

The quiet man from Maine took over the reins from the frenetic young man from Greenwich, Connecticut, when they rode into the show-jumping ring to collect the first-place award. Shaffner and the other Blonde Bombers were second. Michael's team was third and Best's New Jersey Knights were fourth.

No one planned to switch equestrian careers based on their performances in the Challenge of Champions. However, it was a change, and that goes a long way with riders who do the same thing over and over with only the place changing from week to week.

That Saturday, June 22, would decide the USET's show-jumping championship. It would also be the final selection trial for the Pan American team. And the day was to offer a glimpse into the future: the Rolex/USET Talent Derby showcasing riders who might ride for the team in the twenty-first century.

On the day before, Michael had won the $15,000 qualifier for the $50,000 Cadillac/USET Show Jumping Championship on Rhum IV, an eight-year-old French horse owned by Yolanda Garcia Cericeda. Afterwards, talking to the press, Michael declared the horse "our new Jet Run." It seemed as though he was on his way to his third straight win in the USET championship, won the year before at the Hampton Classic in storybook fashion. He had also won the title in 1981, 1983 and 1989.

There were other reasons for optimism to run through the Vintage Farm personnel at the show just two hours away from home. D. D. and Bon Retour had done well in the qualifier, and her hopes of representing the U.S. in Havana were bright. Dina Santangelo also still had the opportunity to make the Pan Am squad. Finally, Lisa Jacquin and the aging but still brilliant For The Moment had done well and had a shot for the championship. All had made the cut, all would ride in the next day's grand prix.

If Michael had reason to rejoice, then Tony Font had reason to be dejected. On Friday, before the qualifier, Lego stepped from his stall in the tent lame. There was an abscess on his right front hoof, nothing life threatening but enough to keep him from competing.

A comparatively minor injury scuttled the chances of this pair—considered by most to be the best in the hunt for a spot on the team—for riding in Havana. It also undid the best human interest story of the Games.

Font was four years old when his parents fled Castro's Cuba. Now their son, an American, a Texan no less, was on the verge of a triumphant return. But Tony and Martha Font watched as their son loaded Lego onto his trailer. They had come to Gladstone to see him ride, and left even before the young riders of the Talent Derby had a chance to walk the course.

It was a mercifully short drive from USET headquarters at Gladstone to James Young's farm in New Hope, Pennsylvania. Lego stayed there for a while. It was okay. Font had planned a break in the summer. This would be it.

Font soaked Lego's foot. Finally he found the abscess and had it opened to drain.

"If something can go wrong with them, it will," he said. "Sometimes it just happens at the wrong time."

As if enough hadn't already gone wrong, Font sustained another loss. While at Young's, Sarah, one of Font's dogs, ran into the road, was struck by a car and had to be put down.

Elsewhere, the first weekend of summer was beginning to look as though it might be perfect, and that the inaugural Festival of Champions had been spared the horse-show curse of rain. It was a fitting setting for Schuyler Riley and Flamingo to make history. In the seven years of the Rolex/USET Talent Derby, this nineteen-year-old Tufts University student became the first woman to win the class. In second was another woman, Wendy Chapot. In fact, only three of the twelve ribbons in the $15,000 Talent Derby went to men.

Kate finished eighth in the Talent Derby with Hearsay, Mr. Dependability. She had the second fastest time of the 4-faulters, undone by knocking down a rail on the very last fence. She and Ginsing had 12 faults and were out of the ribbons.

The Talent Derby had gone off under near perfect conditions. It was bright and breezy. But by the 2:00 P.M. start of the USET championship, it had cooled and a light drizzle made the Barbours blossom. It wasn't long, however, before even the venerable deep green, waxed-cotton jackets that are de rigueur in equestrian sports were of little help. The drizzle had become a downpour and the perfect summer day had turned November-like.

That was not the cheeriest of prospects for the field of riders facing, not the customary one round before a jump-off, but two. Pine Meadow soon became Pine Meadow Marina by the time of the jump-off. The format for the class required riders to be clear in the two rounds in order to make it to the jump-off. Many were unable to accomplish that. Michael and Rhum IV were clear in the two rounds but withdrew. So did Debbie Dolan on Arrangeur, and George Lindemann, Jr. on Lari 326.

Jacquin and Best watched much of the class from under a golf umbrella they shared. They compared notes on holding onto the reins in the rain. They both cursed the cold rain, which by the end of the second round made it impossible to see one end of the ring from the other.

Surprisingly, only one rider fell during the afternoon. Dina Santangelo, fighting for a final clear and a berth on the Pan American team, crashed the final fence. The twenty-seven-year-old woman who trained with Michael parted company with Aramix, falling heavily and headfirst into the mud. One group of riders and grooms at the in-gate went after the horse. Michael led the group of others who went to Dina's aid. Eventually she was able to stand and was assisted from the ring, Michael at her side. A medical exam later showed she had received a concussion.

In the end, three riders made it to the jump-off: Jacquin on For The Moment, Michael Dorman on Olisco and Rich Fellers on El Mirasol.

One of Ronnie Beard's grooms ran back to the stabling tents to get a different—more importantly, dry—saddle for Dorman. After the change, Dorman sat amidst a sheet of steam coming off the eleven-year-old Selle Français as he reviewed the jump-off course. Beard held a copy up for him to see, but soon it disintegrated in the rain.

Finally, the tall, slender, soft-spoken thirty-four-year-old rode into what had become a lake with eight jumps standing above its waters. He emerged clear, but his exacting approach gave him a time of 47.483 seconds, .483ths of a second over the time allowed.

Fellers, a thirty-one-year-old from Diamond Bar, California, went next, the red from his hunt coat bleeding into the white of his britches. He and the 17-hand, nine-year-old Thoroughbred picked their way through the puddles in what would prove to be the fastest time among the three finishers, 39.493, easily avoiding the time faults that had hurt Dorman and Olisco. However, they had 4 faults.

It was left to Jacquin and For The Moment to try for a clear round within the 47 seconds allowed. She worked the edges of the jumps, trying to avoid the chewed-up and soaked paths the others had taken. Even that proved difficult; she just about came off over the neck of the big horse. Every effort had become a water jump, not a simple liverpool, but a lake, the kind three-day-event riders plunge into.

In the end, the transplanted—and nearly frozen—Arizonan won. Jacquin was clear in 44.958 over a course she could barely see amid the downpour.

"If I hadn't had a nice horse I would have died," said Jacquin to Michael at the in-gate after the victory. Later she'd say, "I was sliding all over the place. All I could do was aim at the jump."

Later, Jacquin said she was shocked by the performance of For The Moment: "He's very funny about footing. He likes a very firm, secure takeoff. The second round made me nervous, he slipped a couple of times, and I thought, oh, gosh, it's not going to be good, but I was amazed that he kept going. He was wonderful to do what he did."

Jacquin was the latest USET show-jumping champion. The sloppy, soggy Saturday also decided who would go to Havana to represent the U.S. in the Pan American Games.

Feller's double clear before the jump-off had allowed him to complete the Pan Am trials routine as the top finisher with no faults. The remainder of the team would be D. D. and Bon Retour, who had finished the two rounds that day with three-quarters of a time fault; Andre Dignelli of Bedford, New York, on Gaelic, and Debbie Shaffner—who earlier in the month had won the Happy Valley Grand Prix in Centre Hall, Pennsylvania, on Texas T—with Poor Richard.

Afterwards Michael stood, soaked, in the tack stall waiting for D. D. As a freshly minted USET member preparing for international competition, she had to undergo mandatory drug testing. She, along with Shaffner, Fellers and Dignelli drank fruit juice and waited at the Team headquarters. Michael chatted with John Cowan, his young rider who had 4-faulted the first round of the Talent Derby. Both had searched without luck for a bootjack, so they stood with clammy, cold boots on their feet as they admired a puppy from a litter by D. D.'s dog Daisy, and waited.

Jacquin also wanted to get dry and warm, but her victory was a suitable substitute. She took off her helmet and hairnet, shaking free long, brown hair that framed her smile. She happily fed carrots to For The Moment, nuzzling, talking to him, a proud mother adoring a precocious son.

For a woman who has risen to the top of the sport, ridden on the silver medal–winning American teams at the 1987 Pan American Games and the 1988 Olympics, For The Moment was the only horse Lisa Jacquin had ever owned. Even at that, Jacquin had to borrow the $25,000 to buy Fred, as he is known in the barn.

Jacquin grew up in Tucson in a family of lawyers involved in Arizona Republican politics in those comparatively calm days before Evan Mecham arrived at the State House. Her father William, friend of Barry Goldwater, had been lieutenant governor under Jack Williams in the late 1960s and early 1970s, had served as president of the Arizona State Senate for ten years and once ran for governor. Her mother Deborah had served as a county attorney. Today her parents operate Issue Management Inc., a governmental affairs firm in Phoenix. Her brother Greg is the minority leader in the Arizona State Senate, and sister Susan had worked for Gov. Bruce Babbitt.

"Whenever anyone asks them what I did, they say, 'Oh, she plays with horses,'" laughed Jacquin, who the week before had won the $50,000 Michelob Upperville (Virginia) Jumper Classic, edging Katie Monahan Prudent and Silver Skates in a three-rider jump-off rounded out by Anne Kursinski and Mirco.

Jacquin began riding at a small neighborhood lesson barn. It was there she was seen by Kaye Love, the woman who would become her trainer, mentor and pseudo-parent when Jacquin went to live with her at the age of eleven so she could concentrate on riding.

Eventually Jacquin made the major migration east. She rode with George Morris, riding with Louie Jacobs and Joan Scharffenberger on a junior team he took to Europe in 1978. Afterward she worked four years for Leslie Burr Lenehan in Fairfield, Connecticut. She graduated from the University of Southern California with a political science degree and a minor in psychology.

It was while she was working for Lenehan that she began looking for a horse. Instead she found a soul mate in the 15.3-hand bay Thoroughbred she bought as a seven-year-old, two years after he had finished a racing career at a lot of small tracks.

The son of the Calumet Farm stud Celebration was a little skinny when Jacquin, then twenty, first saw For The Moment in 1982. "Just a horse," said Jacquin.

He also was a little spunky, still carrying the chip on his withers typical of many racing Thoroughbreds. That was a trait which endeared him to Lenehan.

The deal was made.

"It didn't take long for him to settle down," said Jacquin. "He wanted to be a good horse. Now he's a winner, and there aren't a lot of horses that want to win the way he does."

His first grand prix win came in 1984. It was the grand prix of the Los Angeles International. It was a World Cup qualifier.

"It was huge," said Jacquin. "I was terrified. Fred wasn't. He jumped so high and careful."

That was the beginning of a string of grand prix victories in seven years. Also, it started a friendship not often seen at this level of competition. Some horses to some riders are clearly vehicles and little else. Any real affection they receive comes from the grooms who prepare them, feed them, bathe them, tack them, worry over them.

Then there is Lisa Jacquin and For The Moment.

"I live for that horse," she said.

*   *   *

Not appearing at the Festival of Champions was one of the winningest riders in show jumping. Also one of the busiest.

Instead of riding Pine Meadows' Elysian fields-turned-lake, Goldstein was riding in Detroit, the hometown of her sponsor, the Cadillac Motor Car Division of General Motors. She had spent a lot of time studying airline schedules trying to work out arrangements to fly from Detroit to Gladstone and back to ride in both events. About the only way it could have worked was to have a private jet to do the chauffeuring, something outside the financial realm of a rider even as successful as Goldstein.

Still, it worked out. Goldstein rode Saluut II to victory in the $50,000 Cadillac Grand Prix of Detroit. It was her third win of the month of June. The week before Goldstein and Saluut II had won the $50,000 Crown Royal Motor City Grand Prix, flying in the morning of the event from the Memphis Classic and riding while the show and surrounding area was under a tornado warning. She also started the month off winning the $30,000 Music City Grand Prix in Nashville on Daydream.

David Raposa was another rider to take a pass at the Festival of Champions. Instead, he and Seven Wonder went to and won the Grand Prix of Roanoke in Salem, Virginia. It was one of the easier $100,000 wins he or any rider could have. Seven Wonder faced only twenty-four other horses, a small field for big money. And with the USET knee deep in mud and celebration and Detroit worshiping a different kind of horsepower for a change, the field of riders wasn't as deep as it might have otherwise been.

That was one of the benefits—at least to the riders—of this embarrassment of grand prix riches on the same June weekend. Sometimes the schedule breaks in your favor.

Raposa is one of the riders on the circuit who need to have those kinds of breaks every now and then. He is on his own, no family money, no trust fund, no patrons keeping him in the saddle. His ten-stall barn is built next to the lesson operation on his mother's White Fox Farm in Clinton, New York, about forty miles east of Syracuse. He does the work there, the stalls, the painting, almost everything but the books, which his sister keeps for him. It would have been nice to ride at Gladstone, but it was more important to show more selectively at a place where he could improve his chance of winning, or at least placing well.

*   *   *

Kate had ridden with Margie at the Crown Royal in Detroit, before she drove east for the Festival of Champions' Talent Derby. That week at the Bloomfield Open Hunt held some special moments for her, ones that were worth as much as any ribbon she might have won.

After Margie and Saluut II won, the show's organizers wanted as grand a finale as could be had that night. They asked Kate to ride Sebastian, on whom Margie had placed second, back into the ring for the ribbon ceremony. Afterwards, out of the ring, on the ground and standing in the clammy post-storm night, Kate was approached by two girls seeking autographs.

"I'm not Margie," she said, not wanting the girls to later look at the signature and be disappointed it was hers and not that of the other petite woman who rode big gray horses.

"We know."

Kate signed and smiled, and with a ribbon and check in hand walked through the mud back to the Gladewinds stalls. It was a relaxed group she found there. Kate luxuriated in the mellow camaraderie created by the night's one/two finish. The storm had broken the back of the heat that had held the showgrounds all day, and left about 110,000 people in the suburbs without electrical power. She replayed the week's successes as she cleaned tack, a calming, lulling repetitious job that goes nicely with easy late-night conversation.

She had been in the low ribbons all week, Ginsing struggling with going over water. Hearsay, Mr. Reliable, was third in two amateur classes. Kate also enjoyed being the owner of Sebastian, watching him regain his form, pinning second that night.

Back at the Guest Quarters Hotel, Kate, Margie and others got a table in the lounge. This was not the normal post-show routine, but there had been success after a hectic pace. Besides, Peter Doubleday had bought champagne. About 2,000 people had watched that win, which included a $15,000 check for first place. That was in contrast to the winner's share of the other grand prix in town that same weekend. Emerson Fittipaldi won $148,000 when he won the Grand Prix of Detroit, the kind with high-priced, high-powered automobiles. His win was witnessed by 43,595 spectators.

There was plenty to toast. Margie, in the month of June alone, had— with the grace of creative airline scheduling and a powerful string of big, gray horses—won four grand prix.

*   *   *

The two shows in Detroit had been somewhat disappointing for Beezie and John. In the first week, it appeared as though Beezie and Northern Magic had the jump-off of the Crown Royal grand prix wrapped up. Then, at the last jump, tight to the sponsors' boxes at ringside, with the pair ahead of Goldstein's leading time, Magic stopped. The refusal cost 3 faults.

"I was tasting victory," said Beezie afterwards. "He had gone well all week, I kind of expected him to do well."

In the end, Beezie was fifth on Magic, sixth on Daydream and eleventh on The Girl Next Door.

The next week Schnapps, which Harry Gill had sent from Michael to John, was sixth, and Gusty Monroe was seventh. Northern Magic, performing in front of his owners from nearby Milford, was eleventh.

The two-week stay in Detroit was a busy one for Beezie and John. A number of their clients live in the Midwest, and most of their amateur clients were at the show as well. When the two of them walked amateur/ owner classes with their clients, they led a large group from fence to fence. They discussed the ins and outs of the course with Barb Wolfe, Barb Gould, Frances Elliott, Pam Deslauriers, and Un Jin and Hyun Jin Moon. It became a relay between John and Beezie and Terry as they prepared, schooled and coached amateurs, with thirteen horses in some of the bigger classes.

In part because of this work load, John's sister Mary Jo was helping out, cleaning tack before flying to England to study for the summer at Oxford.

*   *   *

June ended with the show circuit's nominal summer vacation beginning. But that beginning was a little different than usual; separate vacations were being taken by some.

While some wound their eighteen-wheelers and horse vans through northern New York's Adirondack Mountains to Lake Placid, others went in the opposite direction. Kate and Margie Goldstein joined the growing number of riders who were migrating to, of all places, Pittsburgh. So did Beezie and the crew from John Madden Sales. The Hartwood Show Jumping Festival was in its second year and was enjoying what every product, movie and political candidate craves: good word-of-mouth advertising.

Kate's comments seemed to echo that of many in the fraternity. "We've heard a lot of good things about Pittsburgh. It will be nice for a change."

Katie Monahan Prudent and Silver Skates, the new horse that had carried her to a surprise berth in the American Invitational, won at the $35,000 Bourse Shops/Ascot Range Rover Grand Prix Hartwood at the Hartwood Show Jumping Festival. It was their first grand prix victory together, and Monahan Prudent's first since her 1990 injury.

Hartwood, however, was a disappointment to others. The footing was awful to the point of being dangerous, most riders said.

"It's funny," said Goldstein. "All the people who said how marvelous the show was weren't there."

For Beezie and John, Hartwood was even more of a letdown. Beezie lost a bout with the flu and didn't ride.

Change. Amid the glamour of the show circuit there is the grind. There is a regimen week after week from Wellington, Florida, in January to the National Horse Show in November. Anything that makes that routine less so is welcome. That is why Pittsburgh loomed as a possible alternative for so many riders.

Plus, the first week of Lake Placid had something working against it. The Lake Placid Horse Show Grand Prix was a timed first-round class. If riders didn't have horses capable of going quick and clean, it would be difficult to earn back expenses.

There was something more, though. The two horse shows of Lake Placid had also become a favorite stop of a group with no concern for and even less appreciation of the format under which the grand prix was being run. The federal Immigration and Naturalization Service patrolled the show, ever vigilant for the groom without a green card. With some barns not aggressively checking the credentials of their hired help, there was the risk that these sharp-eyed agents would cart off grooms—who happened to be in the country, mostly from Mexico, illegally—in the middle of a show. It had happened before.

This zealous protection of Lake Placid from illegal aliens seemed to have stemmed from an incident several years earlier. Grooms were playing cards in the tent stalls one night. One of them, filled with bravado and liquor, began brandishing a pistol. It went off and the bullet struck a horse, which had to be destroyed.

This was enough to grab the attention of the INS. Since then, its agents made a point of wandering the stalls and grandstands of the two horse shows in this resort town. Patty Harnois, Kate's trainer, with a Cape Cod accent as thick as the fog rolling in off the Atlantic, once was rousted by agents demanding to see her green card.

Still, Lake Placid was a great place to be as summer began. That had been Leslie Burr Lenehan's outlook for several years. She and Pressurized won the grand prix that first weekend of the Lake Placid shows. It was the seventh time that she had taken the victory gallop in Lake Placid, and the win came a year to the day after Pressurized had been injured while shipping to the show.

As Lenehan and Pressurized won, Anne Kursinski on Starman was becoming the first American in twenty years to win the $125,000 Grand Prix of Aachen. The last U.S. rider to win the class watched by 48,000 spectators was Neal Shapiro and Sloopy, who tied with France's Marcel Rozier in 1971.

It was the biggest win for the thirty-two-year-old California native, who had finished fourth at the 1988 Olympics. Also, it turned out to be one of the highlights for Americans riding abroad in 1991.

*   *   *

Elsewhere, Paul Greenwood and Robin Bacon were married on the grand prix field of his Old Salem Farm in North Salem, New York, she arriving in a horse-drawn carriage. Afterward the couple cruised to Europe on the *Queen Elizabeth II*.

In Gainesville, Florida, and elsewhere around the country, defense attorneys were, in the vernacular of the law, deposing witnesses in the case against Tommy Burns and Harlow Arley in the February death of Streetwise. A trial date in the middle of July was expected.

CHAPTER 9

Summer Vacation
...Almost

The score was David Raposa's and Jimmy Torano's softball team 23 and Eric Hasbrouck's squad 13.

But there was consolation for Hasbrouck. The thirty-one-year-old native of Washington State—and unofficial social director during the two weeks East Coast show jumping encamps in northern New York's Adirondack Mountains—won the fishing derby. Hasbrouck, who a month earlier had won the sixty-second annual $30,000 Ox Ridge Charity Horse Show on Denizen, took the prize with the fourteen-inch rainbow trout he caught while fly fishing the Ausable River.

Linda Yarborough, an amateur riding here under the eye of Michael, shot the lights out at the skeet shooting contest. She broke twenty-one of twenty-five targets. The young Texan confessed to having shot before.

And just about everyone played in Mudpuddles. This two-level bar on School Street around the corner from American Legion Post 326 was as busy and crowded as the warmup rings at the showgrounds a couple of miles away. When the horse shows come to Lake Placid, the horse-show crowd goes to Mudpuddles, and owner Gary Ottavinia smiles a lot; it's good for business, better than the bobsledders and hockey players in the winter. (More tipping and less pinching, said the waitresses.) Besides, he got to umpire the softball game.

121

Such was Lake Placid, East Coast show jumping's two-week summer camp, a place where horse shows have been held since the early 1930s. The atmosphere was relaxed, though not as laid back as the normal West Coast show, but about as easygoing as it gets for shows east of the Mississippi River and north of the Mason-Dixon Line. People who show here like it that way. Just as Wellington frees many of them from bleak winters, Lake Placid gets them out of the heat of summer and into a lakeside resort community propelled by the energy of athletes and tourists reaching for their Gold Cards.

It was eleven years before that the world focused anew on Lake Placid, a village of 2,485 people first settled in 1850. In 1932 it hosted a Winter Olympics, which in size and scope was a warmup meet compared to the multimillion-dollar extravaganza that overran what is at once one of the poorest parts of rural upstate New York State and its most fashionable tourist enclave. The 1980 Winter Olympics brought a renewed interest in this village, which began life as two large farms, one owned by Joseph Nash and the other by Benjamin Brewster. The Games also brought federal and state money, helping expose the region to the world just when Ronald Reagan's go-go, spend-spend, easy-credit 1980s began to buy now and pay later.

Part of that government money helped build the 70-meter and 90-meter ski jumps about two miles outside the village on Route 73, and just around the corner from where the body of abolitionist John Brown lies a-molderin' in his grave. Across the road and next to a small but busy municipal airport—a former harness racing track—is the Lake Placid Horse Show grounds. When athletes from around the world were here in 1980 thrilling in victory and agonizing in defeat, this was where it all began. The massive torch that burned throughout the Games still stands not far from where horses are stabled.

In the summer of 1991, skiers once again flew down the skyscraping jumps, taking off from a track of water-covered ceramic tiles and landing on a special plastic matting instead of snow. Nearby, in the Kodak Sports Park, airborne freestyle skiers twisted, turned, somersaulted, and landed in a large pool of water.

And across the road, about 750 horses created traffic jams in the warmup rings similar to those that occur daily as thousands of tourist cars wander slowly to find an elusive parking place in the village's shopping district. The Lake Placid Horse Show ran from June 26–30, and after a Monday and Tuesday of recreation, was followed by the I Love New York Horse Show straddling the July Fourth holiday from the third to the seventh.

The mountains of the Sentinel Range linger to the north of the show grounds. When not wearing a stylish but forbidding cloak of clouds, Whiteface Mountain, the downhill skiing venue for the 1980 Games, was a commanding presence. And everywhere there was green, relatives to the trees long ago harvested to build the great camps of the Vanderbilts, the Rockefellers, and Marjorie Merriweather Post.

From Route 73 the ten blue-and-white-striped stabling tents rose like miniature mountains between the show rings and the airport. Across the service drive from them was a clutch of commercial tents, the gypsy-footed folks who tag along from show to show, supplying it with everything from photography to jewelry to frozen yogurt. Next to that, the sponsors' club, a long, low white structure between the grand prix and main hunter rings.

During the week, Beezie and Prost continued their domination of the speed classes. They had three wins on the vast, rolling grand prix ring in Lake Placid.

Beezie attributed her contribution to the string of wins to one thing: "I like to go fast." With a shrug and a smile, a statement at odds with the demeanor of the person saying the words. John is the half of this team who is demonstrative, outgoing, the one who talks, who jokes, who jabs the air with his hands as he speaks. He is the one who formerly raced motorcycles, and the one whose brother, Frank, raced funny cars, mutant machines that scorch quarter-mile drag strips at head-spinning speeds. It is her *grazioso* to his *con spirito*.

Still, she and Prost appeared seamless on the grass grand prix ring of Lake Placid. Prost is one of those rare horses who likes to, and should be, run every day. Do that with most horses, and you create problems. Do it with Prost, and he gets better. He gallops well, doesn't hang in the air too long, making him well suited for speed courses that are large, filled with long runs at single fences.

"Most horses, if you run them, get excited and more and more brave all the time and more aggressive," she said. "You can run Prost to the point where he starts to slow down himself. That's a rare thing. Other horses do that a lot sooner, but they're the real chicken ones. He's brave but sensible too."

For that, Prost and Beezie seemed the ideal match.

*   *   *

On Sunday, July 7, the sponsors' and exhibitors' tables were filled, fresh flowers in the centerpieces. The long holiday weekend boosted the gate, and the ski-jumping competition across the road sent a few folks straggling over to ogle the horses warming up in the roadside schooling ring.

The grand prix had a mercifully early start: 1:00 P.M., giving riders, trainers, and grooms a little extra sunlight in which to pack for the trip to the next show or, for the lucky few, home.

The class today would be without Northern Magic. But that seemed a victory for Beezie and John. The ten-year-old Dutch-bred gelding had continued to struggle. He had not been at the top of his game for several months, and the reasons for this slide were elusive. It was pronounced at Pittsburgh. He seemed to be favoring his left front leg, and not creating the exacting fault-free rounds that had earned Beezie her dramatic win at the National in 1989 and her shot at the World Championships in 1990. But Beezie, John and Dr. John Steele, the farm's veterinarian, could not pinpoint the problem.

Then, at Lake Placid, there came a clue. Northern Magic was lame as he stepped from his stall one day. An abscess on his right rear hoof had finally broken through.

This could have been caused by a bruise picked up but unnoticed months ago. A stone may have hit Magic's foot. It could have been caused by a nail driven slightly too far when a new shoe was put on. Whatever it was, it was like a sliver under the fingernail of a person. Such slight injuries have many causes, and while far from life threatening, they can hinder the performance of a horse, even one as talented as Northern Magic.

Steele told Beezie and John that the abscess may have been brewing for months, and just now in Lake Placid showed itself fully. Possibly, it was causing the horse to cut his stride a bit short, making him appear to favor his left front, when it was the right rear that was hurt.

"Now it's beginning to all make sense to me. Maybe this is the missing link," said Steele, a tall, cheerful man with glasses and an omnipresent baseball cap.

Steele was able to relieve the pressure and pain caused by the built-up fluid in the abscess. To do that thoroughly, Steele had to trim away a large portion of the hoof, down to the laminea, to be sure all of the infection would clear. Removing that much of the hoof meant Northern Magic would not jump for several months. Then, with indoors requiring horses to qualify, the horse was effectively sidelined for the remainder of the year.

*   *   *

Twelve horse-rider combinations went clear in the first round of the $50,000 I Love New York Grand Prix and returned for the jump-off. Early on, it looked as though Leslie Burr Lenehan would sweep the two grand prix at Lake Placid in 1991. She had won the week before, a year to the day after her number one horse, Pressurized, was injured shipping in to the Adirondack resort town. It was the seventh win in Lake Placid for Lenehan.

Then it was time for Gem Twist to go back into the ring. As he does before every grand prix round Gem Twist appears in, Frank Chapot stood near the in-gate of the Lake Placid field. And, just as he does before every ride, Chapot reached out as Greg walked Gem past and tugged the horse's tail. In his hand was one of the horse's tail hairs. While Greg and Gem negotiated the course, Chapot held the long, nearly white hair in his hand as if it were a rosary. It was a talisman to will the horse he had bred, raised and trained over the course Stephens had set for the day.

It worked. They were clear.

"Boy, I needed that one," said a relieved Best afterward. It had been nearly a year since the rollercoaster had climbed to the top for this pair, and the rider was clearly pleased. In between, Gem had been named best horse at the World Championship in Stockholm the year before, and Best had been the USET's top performer, finishing fourth. Still, he hadn't medaled there. Florida was dismal; no invitation to the Invitational. Even a few mumbles by others that something was wrong.

Being Greg Best and riding Gem Twist is not as easy as it looks. No one wins every time out. Even Gem Twist has his off days. Still, that is hard to reconcile against the hope, against the tailor-made image of the handsome young man on the dashing gray horse. They look perfect, so they should be perfect all the time, every time. That's how we like our heroes.

That's obvious when this pair rides into the ring for a grand prix at a place like the Meadowlands. The sound begins when they walk through the in-gate, and follows them as they move around the perimeter of the course. It is a vocal version of The Wave done primarily by teen-age girls and young women. It's followed by the flash attachments on hundreds of cameras firing as they move. The combined effect is one of light and sound, the kind usually reserved for screen or music celebrities. Score a clear round, and the volume of the screams and the number of flashes doubles.

Simply put, Greg Best and Gem Twist have star quality.

This is not lost on the twenty-seven-year-old from Annandale, New

Jersey. Neither is the fact that it was a long time between victory gallops until Lake Placid.

"It's the biggest charge to hear all of that," he said. "Gem gets as warm a reception as any horse in this country. I get goose bumps just thinking about it. I remember what it was like to cheer like that for Rodney [Jenkins] or Frank."

Still, he couldn't afford to get swept away, to read too much into the ovations, or overreact to them.

"I don't let the pressure get to me," said Best, who usually wears the smile of a man who had something occur to him that was amusing—not funny—but just amusing. "When I have a bad day, I don't worry about it. When I have a great day, I enjoy it. But things are never as good as your best days or as bad as your worst ones."

Best had nearly an entire lifetime to develop that philosophy. He began riding young, growing up on the circuit and with a mother who gained her own share of the spotlight as a trainer and instructor.

By the age of fifteen, Best was already showing jumpers with Frank Chapot, a living legend in the history of the USET and the man who brought Gem Twist to his near-godlike position in the equine world. At home, Chapot had been riding the horse, sired by Good Twist. Best was a sophomore at the University of Pennsylvania at the time.

Chapot, like many riders, had back problems. Gem jumped so high over fences that it was hard on Frank's back.

"So, it was dumb luck," said Best that in 1983 he was to be paired with this superhorse.

Besides, Gem could be something less than super at home.

"He's a nag to ride on a regular basis, a plug," he said. "At home he's like lugging a sack of potatoes around the field.

"But walk into a show ring and he just gets pumped up. Still, he knows the difference between a Wednesday afternoon power and speed class and a Sunday afternoon grand prix, and that's something you can't teach a horse."

Gem Twist was twelve years old when he won the grand prix on the spacious green field in Lake Placid. He had already been the AGA Horse of the Year in 1987 and 1989, and placed third for that honor in 1988. He and Best won the individual silver medal at the 1988 Olympics in Seoul, South Korea, and a silver medal at the Pan American Games the year before. Gem was named, appropriately enough, Best Horse at the World Championship in Stockholm in 1990. The pair won the American Invitational in 1989 and the AGA Championship in 1987.

Karl Leck's photograph of Gem and Greg jumping through the Korean gate at the Seoul Olympics has become one of the enduring images of the sport. The two were immortalized with a poster of their own, something usually reserved for the athletes and swimsuit models from *Sports Illustrated* and rock stars. The Miller's Harness Co. catalog featured Best with several female models, all wearing clothing from a collection licensed by the USET. Best drives a bright red Porsche, and sometimes has to fend off the advances of admiring women. If the sport has a recognizable public persona, it is this pair.

And therein lies the problem of being Greg Best and riding Gem Twist, one of the few $3 million horses in the world.

"I'm not bragging, but I've already done it all," says Best. "The Olympics. The World Cup. The World Championship. What else is there to do? I already hit the top and there's only one way to go, and I'm only twenty-seven. I could spend the next thirty years beating my head against the wall and never achieve what I've already done.

"Who knows, maybe I'll be twice as lucky as I already have been and find another Gem Twist in the next thirty years, but who knows? It's nice to know I went to school."

*   *   *

Michael and Heisman finished eighth in the grand prix at Lake Placid. The stay in the resort town hadn't been a complete vacation. The days were filled with hard work—several amateurs with several horses each. All needed to be schooled, watched, prepared, critiqued, readied for the next class and the next day.

Then again, it was shot through with an element, an energy usually missing at such shows. It is a presence usually even missing in the simpler days of life at the farm in Collegeville: Mikey and Michelle were with their dad. They usually live with their mother near Montreal. Lake Placid is an annual opportunity to see Dad work, and much more.

Lake Placid's horse shows were their own massive playgrounds. The orbits of their play would take them close to Michael and then sling them through the stabling areas, around the hunter ring and into the sponsors' tent. But, always, several times each morning and afternoon, they'd drift back to Michael's side, Mikey on one side, Michelle on the other, arms around his waist as he watched one of his amateurs ride. Then they were off, playing with someone's dog, or one of the children of another rider.

On the day of the grand prix, Michael had plenty of help when he walked the course. Mikey and Michelle were at his side. Most of the way, Michelle held her father's hand as they walked among the obstacles set by Steve Stephens. At one point, Mikey tried valiantly to count strides between the jumps, stretching long behind his father and falling behind every now and then, running to catch up and resume his pacing.

Clearly smitten by his children, Michael is worried he's not there enough for them. They live in Montreal. He in Pennsylvania. Visits are frequent, but are only visits. He worries too that they are not there enough for him, and worries about even having that feeling.

The horse-show world is hard on families, hard on relationships. Scheduling is absurd. Travel ridiculous. Michael said that is what did in his marriage. It is an immersion in a world of rapid accelerations and abrupt stops. Because of this, there are many marriages of one rider to another: Leslie Burr and Brian Lenehan, Michele McEvoy and Tim Grubb, and Katie Monahan and Henri Prudent. And many are the children who grew up on the circuit and as adults decided to stay. Even this is no guarantee for success or marital bliss.

*   *   *

An incident in Lake Placid afforded a little more insight into these athletes, these show jumpers at or near the top of their sport, envied, adored, worshiped.

On the Saturday before the big amateur classes, tall, muscular men stretched near the ring, hanging their heels over the white three-rail fence along the driveway of the showgrounds. They ran in place, lifting their legs chest high, and then would ease off in a gentle jog.

A group of riders and trainers hung near the in-gate speculating.

"Isn't that Herschel Walker?" said one.

"Yes, it is."

"No, it isn't. But I know that's Edwin Moses."

It was Edwin Moses, the closest thing to a perfect athletic performer as has been seen in the Olympics. He still owns a lengthy string of undefeated performances in the hurdles.

Moses, tall, slender, wearing thin-rimmed blue, circular glasses, was in Lake Placid not to run hurdles, not even to train for that event. Instead, he and Willie Gault, a track star turned football player, and Gary Harrell, a tight end for the Los Angeles Raiders of the National Football League, were among the mountains of northern New York to try out for yet another sport: bobsledding. Moses, Gault, Harrell (and later Walker, also of the NFL) were in town for the competition used to decide who would push the four-man sled in the Winter Games of 1992 in Albertville, France.

After their workout, the three athletes wandered over to the show ring. It wasn't long before they were besieged by spectators, hounded for autographs and finally on horseback. Three suitable mounts appeared, and Moses, Gault and Harrell were in the show ring. Ideally, they were to have walked and waved. Instead, they trotted, and Gault had his horse into a canter. That they didn't attempt the jumps was a miracle, and no doubt a source of relief for whoever had written the liability insurance for the show.

At the end of the impromptu demonstration, Moses made a springing dismount from his horse, drawing a round of applause. This bit of athletic cross-pollination ended in a group photo: Moses, Gault, Harrell and just about every rider who could crowd around them. As shutters clicked, each group of athletes spoke admiringly of the talents of the other.

Then, things got back to normal, or as normal as things ever are at a horse show.

(Oddly enough, as if taking a cue from show jumping, the efforts of Moses, Gault and Harrell to push the bobsled in the Olympics wound up in court.)

* * *

The two-week respite that was the Lake Placid stop on the East Coast show-jumping tour ended. Taken together, the two weeks of Lake Placid were down from the past year primarily because the first week of the show had gone head to head with the second year of a major show in Pittsburgh. Many riders had gone there, skipping the first week of Lake Placid in favor of a show that had received incredible reviews in its 1990 inaugural year.

Beezie was among the riders at the Pittsburgh show known as the Hartwood Show Jumping Festival. She had the flu and did little riding, but agreed with John's assessment that the footing had been bad. Bad enough in fact to make some say that they'd not go back.

Others, like Alice Debany, had skipped both Pittsburgh and Lake Placid. She and The Natural were in Spruce Meadows, the premier facility in Calgary, Alberta. They won the $50,000 CIBC North America Grand Prix. Barney Ward was second on Watch Out, and Darlene Sandlin and Alley Oop were third.

Beezie and John originally had planned to leave Lake Placid for a southern swing . . . an extreme southern swing of shows. They were to travel to Argentina with the Moon children for a series of shows in Argentina. However, plans didn't materialize, so like many in the East Coast show-jumping fraternity, they instead went west.

Later in the month Peter Leone and Crown Royal Oxo won the $35,000 Michelob U.S. Open Jumping Championship in Moreland Hills. In the Green Mountains of Vermont, Kursinski won the $25,000 Vermont Classic II on Cannonball, and was third on Mirco. And, in Colorado, Tracy Feeney and Infinity, the surprises of the Pin Oak Charity Horse Show in April, picked up their first grand prix victory at the $25,000 Johnny Walker event in Parker.

Also, Michael picked up his first grand prix victory of the year. He and Heisman had a deliberate, clear round to win the $75,000 Prudential Securities American Jumping Classic in Kings Mills, Ohio, home of the College Football Hall of Fame.

But it was a narrow victory. Heisman had dropped a rail at the second-to-last jump-off fence, and the scoreboard flashed 4 faults for the pair; it looked as if Joe Fargis and Mill Pearl had won. Michael appealed, and the jump crew quickly identified that the rail that had fallen was not the top one, and Michael was ruled the winner.

It was not a particularly easy grand prix. The footing in the Galbreath Field football stadium may be used to the abuse it gets from halfbacks and fullbacks, but it turned slick when it was Thoroughbreds and Warmbloods doing the pounding.

Fargis, Jacquin, who was third with For The Moment, and Goldstein and Saluut II went fast in the jump-off round. Each wound up with 4 faults on the Richard Jefferies course. Michael turned in a clear time about five full seconds slower than that of Fargis and Mill Pearl.

It was a win worth celebrating. What wasn't celebrated, however, was July 19. The day went unnoticed, uncelebrated and unobserved. Despite the fact it was an anniversary of sorts for D. D. and him, there was no hint of celebration.

On that day in 1989, Michael and D. D. were returning from Hawaii. He had judged a horse show there and given one of the few clinics he does. They were heading home. Their flight to the mainland was delayed two hours, causing them to miss a connecting flight in Denver. Because of this, they wound up on United Airlines Flight 232 from Denver to Chicago and then on to Philadelphia. They were the last two people to board, getting the only remaining seats: D. D. in row 9 right behind first class, and Michael in row 15, just ahead of the wings of the McDonnell Douglas DC-10-10 jumbo jet.

At 3:16 P.M. (CST), as a film about the Triple Crown flickered across the plane's screen, there was a loud metallic clank. The fifteen-year-old wide-bodied plane, flying a bit more than seven miles above the earth, dipped a little in the air over western Iowa. Chicago was only an hour away, but it may as well have been on the other side of the world.

The sound was that of one of the turbofan disc assemblies breaking loose in the number-two engine, the one positioned in the tail of the aircraft. The broken metal became supersonic knives, slashing through the tail section of the plane, severing the hydraulic lines of the aircraft.

A minute later, Captain A. C. Haynes reported to a Federal Aviation Agency control center in Minneapolis that Flight 232 had lost all hydraulic power. Flaps, slats, ailerons, elevators and rudders—the mechanisms used to steer the plane—were immobilized. A McDonnell Douglas DC-10-10 was designed with three hydraulic systems, one powered by each engine, and can continue normal flight with the loss of one such system. Losing two would make the aircraft difficult to maneuver. However, the loss of all three systems was considered so remote a possibility that it wasn't even covered in the aircraft's emergency procedures manual. Having a fan blade slash through all three hydraulic systems was, in fact, a billion-to-one proposition.

Fortunately, Captain Haynes was probably the most qualified pilot on United's staff to be at the controls that bright summer day over the cornfields of western Iowa. For thirty-three of his fifty-eight years, the gray-haired Haynes, a man with equal loves for umpiring Little League baseball games and flying DC-10s, had been aloft for United. Calling on every second of training and experience he had, Haynes managed to keep panic out of the cockpit, the plane in the air, and maneuver it toward the Sioux Gateway Municipal Airport in the extreme southwest corner of Iowa. As he did, air traffic controllers pinpointed small airports and even sections of four-lane highway where the plane might land if necessary.

By alternating power to the remaining two engines, one on each wing, Haynes, First Officer William Records, Second Officer Dudley Dvorak and Dennis Fitch, a United pilot flying as a passenger on Flight 232 who had joined the cockpit crew to help, were able to "steer" the plane by making only right turns. It was an incredible feat, something even the most experienced pilots have trouble doing, even on the ground in flight simulators.

At 3:40 P.M. Haynes circled the airport at Sioux City and warned the passengers to prepare for an emergency landing. D. D. and Michael, like the other 294 passengers on board, leaned forward in their seats, putting their heads between their knees and cupping their hands behind their heads.

To the hundreds of emergency and medical personnel assembled near Runway 22 at Sioux Gateway, the approach of United Flight 232 looked normal, a bit fast but normal. In fact, the DC-10 was bearing down on the runway at more than 215 knots, much faster than for a normal landing. Then, just a few hundred yards away from the airport, the massive airliner, then about twenty feet above the ground, made a slight correction to the left, then dipped to the right. Haynes was helpless to keep the wing tip from catching the ground, sending the DC-10 into a flaming cartwheel that left a path of wreckage a mile and a half wide across the runway and into a nearby field of corn six feet high.

In the crash, the plane broke into five parts. The first class compartment disintegrated, and the coach portion behind the wing was destroyed. Landing intact were several rows ahead of the tail, the cockpit, and that section of coach seating behind the first-class bulkhead and ahead of the wing—the section in which D. D. and Michael had been belatedly and separately seated.

That section, however, flipped, skidded and came to a smoldering rest in the corn upside down, suspending passengers in their seats. When it finally came to rest, D. D., Michael and the other passengers hurriedly unbuckled their seatbelts, toppling to the ceiling, which was now the floor. There was a scramble to get out and away from the section of fuselage, which was beginning to fill with acrid black smoke.

Flight 232 had an inordinately large number of children on board that day. The airline was promoting a plan that allowed children younger than twelve to fly for free when with their parents on a Tuesday or Wednesday. This Wednesday in July there were plenty of children aboard. Michael didn't leave the wreckage until he had helped two, a boy, and a girl the same age as his daughter Michelle, escape. Then he held up cables so others could make their way free of the mangled plane.

Then came the nerve-wracking task of trying to find D. D. Michael circled the wreckage, looking for her distinctive long, red hair and the bright yellow suit she was wearing for the flight home. He couldn't find her. When the part of the plane they were in finally came to a halt, she had bolted, running almost a quarter mile into the tall, green cornfield before stopping.

Michael continued to help in the rescue efforts. D. D. and he were finally reunited, and they were among the passengers treated and released the same day from one of several hospitals that had received the injured. He had a broken ankle. She had no serious injuries. They were among the 184 people who somehow survived the crash of United 232. In all, 112 people died that deadly day in Iowa.

Later D. D.'s sister arrived in Sioux City on a private plane from Texas to ferry the pair home to Pennsylvania.

That weekend they skipped the show in Cleveland, but on the last Sunday of the month, Michael rode Schnapps, winning the $75,000 Gucci/Hampton Classic Grand Prix at Southampton, Long Island. D. D. won a big amateur class. George Vecsey devoted his Sunday column in the *New York Times* that week to Michael's heroism, and the ABC Nightly News made him its "Person of the Week." It took having one of its brightest stars almost killed in an air disaster to get the kind of media attention that baseball, football, golf and even soccer can count on receiving daily. Even for a man who had competed in the Olympics, won six Pan American medals, won two world championships and earned more money than everyone in the sport save one man.

But the time in the spotlight was minor compared to what else Michael escaped from that burning plane with. The win at Southampton was even less.

Something that escapes most people even unto death was Michael's after July 19, 1989. Call it insight. Call it perspective. Call it what you will, it changed this man who by his own admission could be stiff-necked, touched with a bit of "the Dutch," as Harry Gill once said.

"Hey, it's only show jumping," Michael would say, his head tilted, a knowing smile on his face, sharing an immutable truth, a secret that he didn't want to keep. It was something that had eluded him until he faced an obstacle much larger than the widest oxer, the tallest vertical, the most daunting six-bar class that he or any rider had ever faced. And Michael had won. There, in that field of bad dreams, he gained a second chance, and no one could have been more appreciative. After that, everything was easy; everything was secondary.

When the National Transportation Safety Board in November of 1991 issued the results of its investigation into the crash of United 232, it said there was a flaw in the disc that caused the engine assembly to break apart. The federal panel said routine inspection should have found the problem, which had been in the part since the thirty-two-inch diameter, 370-pound titanium disc was manufactured.

Eleven days after the second anniversary of United Flight 232's fatal voyage, D. D. was boarding a plane again. So was Bon Retour. They had driven from USET headquarters in Gladstone to Stewart Airport in Newburgh, New York. Here, at what was once to be the fourth airport serving metropolitan New York City, the U.S. team for the Pan American Games in Cuba was off to Florida and then on to Cuba. They were part of a team that would see if they could approach what Michael had done in 1975 on Grande, in 1979 on Jet Run and in 1983 on Chef: a bronze, a gold, and a bronze individually, and three team gold medals.

*   *   *

In northern Florida, the trials of the two men involved with the death of Streetwise the previous February were postponed.

Kate Chope and Hearsay during the Rolex Talent Derby at the USET Festival of Champions at Gladstone in June 1991.

Tammy McHugh bathes Hearsay.

Harry Gill, John Madden and Michael Matz at the Lake Placid Horse Show.

Joe Fargis and George Morris at the Autumn Classic, Port Jervis, New York.

Frank Chapot and Greg Best.

Margie Goldstein and Patty Harnois.

John Madden and Beezie Patton discuss strategy with Hun Jin and Hyun Jin Moon.

Beezie Patton and The Girl Next Door.

Katie Monahan Prudent and Debbie Shaffner.

Michael Matz exercises Ping Pong at his home in Collegeville, Pennsylvania.

D. D. Alexander and Michael
Matz share a laugh.

Debbie Shaffner, David Raposa and Greg Best discuss a course at the Lake Placid Horse Show.

Christian Curry.

Karen Golding.

Michael Matz
and Frank
Chapot.

Course designer Steve Stephens.

Lisa Jacquin.

Tim Grubb.

Groom Lynn Hoppel takes it easy as she cools off the legs of Conversation Piece.

Norman Dello Joio.

Canadian jumping star Ian Millar.

Leslie Burr Lenehan after her victory at the Lake Placid Horse Show.

John Madden and Terry Bradner.

Leslie Burr Lenehan and
Pressurized.

The National Horse Show.

CHAPTER 10

Dangerous. Ridiculous. The Year's Best Class

America would have a team at the eleventh annual Pan American Games in Havana, Cuba. It hadn't always seemed it would. Not until the final round of the selection trial did anything seem to be for sure.

In the spring of 1991, it had become the chic thing to do, if you were a show jumper of any caliber, to scoff at the Pan Am Games. There were also some legitimate concerns. However, even after those were set aside, there was a certain aloofness from the Games by most riders. In the end, a handful went through the process and reaped the considerable rewards.

Some riders said their owners didn't want their horses going to Havana, unsure of the equine health conditions on the island nation. Others said they weren't sure horses would get back in the country in time for indoors, or at all, since quarantine requirements remained hazy. Many just didn't want to deal with the heat and humidity of Cuba in August. There were also healthy rumors that the equestrian facilities, even the airport handling equipment, were (1) incomplete, (2) inadequate, (3) unsafe and (4) all of the above. And in these days of objective selection criteria, earning favor by riding for the Team was lessened.

Arching over all of these complaints was a pervasive ennui, one that made the Games seem even less than the step-sister to the Olympics some riders regarded it as. The Pan American Games just didn't seem worthy of many riders.

In the end, it came to be that those riders were not worthy of the Games. For those who made the trip to Havana, what they found was a competition that put to shame the 1987 effort in Indianapolis, and was on a par with just about any event the most veteran among them had seen. Further, it gave those riders and a handful of American spectators a flash of the kind of team spirit that, in the best of all possible selection worlds, should pervade all such competitions.

It was an eclectic team that made the trip to Havana. The squad was made up of Shaffner and Poor Richard, Fellers and El Mirasol, D. D. and Bon Retour, and Dignelli and Gaelic. Frank Chapot would be the chef d'equipe. Others in the small American entourage included Michael; D. D.'s mother, Helen Groves; Shaffner's fiancé, Steve Stephens, Feller's wife, Shelly, and Judy Richter, owner of Coker Farm and Dignelli's boss.

Once there, the Americans found that by dint of hard work, much of it by hand, Havana was ready for the Games, which would attract 18,000 athletes, coaches, visitors and spectators. The Games had become a source of national pride and individual sacrifice, Castro spending an estimated $24 million on housing for athletes alone.

The riders, to a person, praised the efforts of the Cubans, both for their hospitality and for the facilities and level of competition.

"You could not have had a better place for a competition," said D. D. "It was 180 degrees from what we had been led to believe we'd find. I *wanted* to go to Cuba. Everyone downplayed it. It's a real shame that more people didn't make an effort for this.

"Normally, I go in the ring because I love it and I do it for myself and my horses. There, I wanted to do it for the Team, and represent the country."

That's the difference between the Pan American Games and classes in even the biggest shows here in the U.S.

"You're not just competing for yourself, you're also competing for your country," said Michael. "There is nothing better than standing on that podium and hearing your national anthem. It's a great, great feeling knowing you were picked by a selection process and you're there to represent millions of people. That's not an easy task. When you win, you feel like you did well for everyone. When you lose, you feel like you let everyone down."

D. D. also said that she could have done a slightly better job of representing the country in Havana. She tried hard, maybe too hard, and came up with some green errors.

"But that's the only way to get that kind of experience," she said.

Michael, who has ridden numerous times in South America, in the biggest classes in this country and in the show-jumping palaces of Europe, was impressed. With that perspective, he said: "Havana was twenty times better than [1987 in] Indianapolis. Someone spent a lot of time organizing. It was nicer than 75 to 80 percent of the places we show. The footing was very, very good. The athletes' village was as nice or nicer than others in the past. It was a pleasant surprise. I sure wish I would have had a horse to ride when I was down there."

There were fans in the barns to beat back the heat of the day, and a water-purifying system. There were no insects. No military guards. No anti-American protests. The apartments in the athletes' village were adequate, and serviced by maids daily. There were no problems getting horses off the plane and to the equestrian facility. Riders mingled with other American athletes, developing a shared sense of mission. All the awful things that were supposed to occur didn't.

A side benefit was the travel. D. D. and her mother were able to rent a car and see some of the countryside outside of Havana. During the trip they saw a former Soviet missile site, a fort from the 1500s and some of the formerly lavish, now decaying, homes indicative of the wealth that had flourished on the island nation before the revolution. They were among a handful of Americans able to see such sites, able to travel in a country most of their countrymen were not allowed to visit.

In the end, Brazil won the gold, Canada the silver. Shaffner, Fellers, Dignelli and D. D. crowded onto the small yellow metal stand to receive the bronze. There were no Americans at the ceremonies for the individual medal. Canada's Danny Foster and Beth Underhill won the gold and the silver respectively, edging out Brazil's Victor Alves. Dignelli finished a close fourth.

There were some mistakes, some cheap rails, some bad luck. There were also some big courses, ones that veteran designer Stephens said met or exceeded anything he had set for such classes as the $100,000 American Invitational. Moreover, the competition was demanding, The team competition started with a speed round, the two rounds over the same course and a jump-off if necessary. The individual medals were decided on two courses: a standard one and a shorter one with bigger jumps. It was a lot of jumping in a short span of time.

"The experience I got down there will be invaluable," said D. D.

There had been the possibility that Fellers would get more than experience. It seemed he might return home with his first child.

Shelly Fellers grooms for her husband, and had she not been more than eight months pregnant with their first child, she would have flown to Cuba with El Mirasol. Instead, Fellers drew that duty and she took his seat on the flight from Tampa to Havana. Somehow, they made it through the Games without having to make a harrowing dash to a hospital for a late-night delivery, and the USET returned with the same number of members with which it had left Tampa.

For Shaffner, in addition, coming home meant returning with much more than just the bronze Pan American medal to display among the many other awards she has accumulated during a career that began in Syracuse as a child. It was a feeling she normally didn't have after a show, no matter how successful it might have been.

"It was a different feeling of competition than I've ever had," she said. "We were with other athletes. We ate together, went places together, kept track of each other's performances. Normally, we're individuals when we go into the ring. This allowed for team spirit to develop, and that's something that is important, especially for younger riders."

It was also something that ran contrary to the flow of feelings within show jumping as it paused before it closed the summer season and prepared for the grind and glamour of indoors.

*   *   *

Cheering sections are rare at horse shows. Cheering sections of African-American school kids even rarer. Still, there was a group of kids cheering loudly as Joe Fargis rode in an afternoon class at the Hampton Classic Horse Show.

"Go, Joe, go! Go, Joe, go! Go, Joe, Go!" that chant rose in shrill preschool tones. Kathleen Tucker, a retired member of the New York City School Board and executive director and volunteer chaperon for the Bridgehampton Day Care kids joined in. "Go, Joe, go! Go, Joe, go! Go, Joe, go!"

Behind the bleachers where the children shouted were two cheerleaders: Michael and Christian Currey. They convinced the visiting day-care children to help Fargis along. As they cheered louder and louder, Michael and Currey laughed in similarly escalating tones, doubling over.

It was an easy place to be inciteful, an easy place to laugh. August and the long show-jumping season were winding down. The sky was clear.

The sun was out. The fog had burned off. The humidity was slight. The Hampton Classic, New York's summer answer to the National Horse Show, had hit its stride under the watchful eye of Tony Hitchcock, the man hired by the National as its producer come the fall. Some 1,200 horses were in the process of being shown, and New York City's vacationing elite were showing up in the yellow and white tents that bordered two sides of the large grand prix ring. At one of the tables a man with *Business Week* in one hand and a show program in the other, a portable telephone in front of him, said, shaking his head, "I can't believe it took me three hours to get out here from the city." Getting to the Hamptons even as The Season wound down was The Dilemma for many, and it doesn't get any easier on Labor Day when The Horse Show is under way.

Since the early part of this century, there have been horse shows in the Hamptons. Interrupted by two world wars and years of no show, then, twenty years ago, it got back on track, growing in size and popularity, rising to one of the most important and most popular shows. It was in 1977 that the first grand prix was held with Bernie Traurig and Southside winning the $10,000 event. From there, it grew in 1990 to be one of the few $100,000 grand prix in the U.S.

That was the size of the Crown Royal Grand Prix that was helping close the 1991 Hampton Classic, one that had not been disturbed by violent weather . . . barely. Hurricane Bob had blown through a week earlier, leaving the show site without electrical power for five days in the week before 1,200 horses were due to arrive. Its $30,000 first prize was the target of Michael, who had won the event the previous two years, in 1989 on Schnapps and in 1990 on Heisman, his mount for 1991. Not surprisingly, he'd have some company, some talented company. The field of thirty-five horses slated to go in the grand prix that first Sunday of September included Font and Lego, Goldstein on four different horses, Dorman and Olisco, Dignelli and his Pan Am mount Gaelic, Monahan Prudent on the surprising Silver Skates, Tim Grubb on Elan's Two Plus Two, Jacquin and For The Moment, relative newcomer Darlene Sandlin and Alley Oop, and local favorites Fargis on Mill Pearl and Dolan on Arrangeur. Still, he had three shots at winning, three good ones: Heisman, Santangelo's Manassas County and Rhum IV. Michael was well mounted enough to disprove the theory that nature abhors a dynasty.

It was a celebrity-studded crowd that gathered for the grand prix. Wandering through the tents were actors Peter Boyle and Stefanie Powers and "Good Morning, America" host and horse-show mom Joan Lunden. D. D. and Sale Johnson, Heisman's owner, shared conversation with author Tom Wolfe. Also there were Calvin Klein, whose wife Kelly had ridden in the hunters earlier in the week, and taste-maker Martha Stewart. As much as they made for good people-watching, the horses and riders in the grand prix created one of the best classes of the season, one that impressed even the participants.

Beyond the faces one would be likely to see in the Metro section of the *Times* on Sunday, the Hampton Classic also was a draw for major businesses, especially the media and luxury goods. This approach cross-pollinated on grand prix day when the *New Yorker* was host to a party in the tent set up by Cadillac. Ralph Lauren. Ann Taylor. Range Rover. Cartier. W. M inc. Revlon. Rolex. In the Hamptons, summer all but gone, the Hampton Classic was the place to be. Because of this, it made sense for business to be there. More than just about any other show in America, the Hampton Classic has that kind of drawing power.

Before the grand prix got started, show-jumping aficionados had the opportunity to say good-bye to one of its well-known competitors. Lisa Tarnopol retired Revlon Adam, a sixteen-year-old Thoroughbred. The pair had won the $50,000 Garden State Grand Prix earlier in the year, and competed in twelve Nations Cup events.

Conrad Homfeld's course on the grass expanse of the Hampton Classic grand prix field at first seemed hard to read. Font and Lego went first, and had a perfect round in the works until they grabbed 4 faults with a foot in the water at the water jump. Then came Goldstein and Aristo, not necessarily the horse among her three entries considered the likely candidate to post the day's first clear. They rapped the Cartier jump hard, but somehow it stayed up.

"I can't believe it," said Harnois as Margie walked from the ring, a grin as wide as the water jump on her face. "The one we told you not to put in this class goes clear!"

Spank, holding Saluut II for his go nine spots later, said to the gray stallion: "You better watch out, pal, or you'll lose your status."

Three horses later, Terry Rudd, reunited with P.S. Gazpacho, the nine-year-old Westphalian, after sitting out a year-long AHSA-imposed suspension for using a banned drug on a horse, ensured the crowd of a jump-off. After that, Anne Kursinski and Mirco, the pair that had placed third at a grand prix in Vermont during July, made it three for the encore. McLain Ward, the fifteen-year-old *wunderkind* and the Oldenburg Just Wait just missed the jump-off, taking a rail at the water wheels oxer.

Saluut II must have listened to the friendly advice of Spank. The stallion, despite shaking the top rail at the oxer in front of the in-gate, was clear, giving Goldstein yet another shot at the $30,000 first-place purse. Michael and Heisman, warmly welcomed by the crowd, followed suit, also getting lucky when the eleventh fence bounced but stayed in place. Dismounting, Michael did a television interview with Mark Leone, and then as he got up on Manassas County, Joan Scharffenberger came over and said, "I have to give out that champagne to the winner, and it would make me very happy to hand it to you."

Four rides later, Fargis and Mill Pearl posted a clear round greeted with great enthusiasm from his hometown fans. Peter Leone matched that with a sponsor-pleasing ride on Crown Royal's Oxo, the 16.2-hand chestnut gelding on which he had posted five wins in five outings.

Michael bought some insurance with Manassas County. He piloted the 17-hand Thoroughbred around Homfeld's course without penalty. The horse was a bit edgy at the start but settled down about a third of the way into things.

Dorman and Sundrum went clear, and it looked as though Goldstein and Sebastian would be too, but picked up a rail and ¼ time fault. Dignelli and Gaelic went clear, as did Grubb and Elan's Two Plus Two. Michael's bid to go three for three missed as Rhum IV had 8 faults.

"He showed his inexperience," Michael told Yolanda Garcia Cericeda, Rhum IV's owner after, standing in the warmup ring. "He got nervous when he heard the plastic of the liverpool ripple."

The jump-off would go off with twelve horse-rider combinations hoping to complete the course before the distant rain got closer. Michael and Heisman flew the course, nearly taking a tumble when Heisman stumbled and had a rail at the last fence.

Kursinski and Mirco went clear. So did Goldstein and Saluut II, shaving about a second off Kursinski's time. Leone and Oxo gave it a terrific shot, slipping ahead of Goldstein by .09 of a second.

In the end, it came down to four experienced riders on experienced horses.

Fargis and Mill Pearl were the first of the last four to go. Mill Pearl, the 17-hand Irish-bred mare, blasted around the course. She stayed balanced, and Fargis kept her at a gallop and posted a round of 46.82, moving Goldstein and Saluut II down a notch.

"Beatable?" said Peter Leone to brother Mark.

"You've got to give it a shot."

He did, the sixteen-year-old gelding trying its best to keep his string of victories intact. Leone was clear but off the supersonic pace of Fargis and Mill Pearl, at 48.07.

"Damn close," said Mark to Peter.

"I should have had it."

The crowd that packed the grandstand drew a collective breath and grew silent as Michael and Manassas County trotted out for their shot at Fargis's time. It seemed to be the best that could be taken. They moved effortlessly from jump to jump, Santangelo standing near the in-gate, fists clenched, rising on her toes as her horse and her mentor took each fence, only relaxing when the pair cruised through the timers and the crowd exploded. The spectators' cheering died when the timer flashed the time: 47.25, .43 of a second off the time of Fargis and Mill Pearl.

"That's dangerous and ridiculous," said a seemingly relieved Michael as he rode over to where Dina stood waiting.

"That was great, Michael," she said. "Just great. I really appreciate it."

The tension had time to mount as Dorman and Sundrum went, taking 4 faults. Dignelli and Gaelic made the decision to go clear instead of fast; they finished in 55.09.

During those rounds, Michael and Grubb played a little verbal volleyball.

"I don't think I can go that fast," said Grubb between drags on a cigarette.

"Then skip a fence," Michael suggested.

Fargis stood under the canopy that formed the in-gate. His arms were folded, his face devoid of emotion.

The British expatriate was about to take his crack at it. He was into the ring with the last bits of his wife's advice trailing him.

"I'm going to have to go like hell," Grubb said to his wife Michelle before he left.

"Even hell might not do it," said Michael, shaking his head and moving to the rail to watch Grubb.

The massive nine-year-old Irish-bred ate up the course. Grubb looked more like a jockey than a grand prix rider, and it looked as though their collaboration would pay off.

But, as the scoreboard clock flashed on, Denise Cojuangco was jumping up and down, pointing to Fargis, her instructor, and screaming, "You did it! You did it!"

He had. Grubb and Elan's Two Plus Two completed the jump-off course in 46.97, .15 of a second behind Fargis.

"That's as fast as I want to go," said Grubb as he dismounted.

The biggest class of the summer had the best finish. Only 3.07 seconds separated the top six finishers. Michael couldn't "three-peat" at the Hampton Classic, but still had two horses in the top ten. Fargis, forty-three, a two-time Olympic medalist, won in front of local fans. The rain had held off. The stands were packed. The tents bristled with the electricity of excitement.

As Fargis was composing himself to talk with Peter Leone for television, Michael stood behind the cameraman. Then, carefully, he placed his thumbs in his ears, waggled his fingers and gave Fargis a loud Bronx cheer.

"There, take that," Michael laughed, once again the cheerleader, of sorts, for Fargis.

*   *   *

Before arriving in the Hamptons, Kate had posted a big win at the Attitash, New Hampshire, Equine Festival. She and Hearsay won the high junior amateur/owner class.

Still, it wasn't enough. She was beginning to feel frustrated by not having done better, not progressed farther, not ridden in more grand prix.

At Southampton, she knew the grand prix would be a beast of a class. Still, when this year dedicated to riding began, she had figured it was possible that she'd be there, that she'd be able to ride in the grand prix and turn in a decent performance. It didn't happen. She knew she wasn't going in the grand prix, so focused on the $25,000 Talent Derby.

Thinking about that class, Kate figured she had as good a shot as anyone in it of being part of the last horse-rider combination to leave the ring. She focused on it. Granted, it was a tough course, but nothing beyond her; no freebies, but nothing killer even.

Kate and Hearsay finished tenth.

McLain Ward had won it. He also finished second.

"I felt like I had a really good shot at it," said Kate. "So it was even more frustrating."

The week of Southampton also signaled a slight change in schedule. Kate left the show on the third day to register for the genetics class she had to take at Brown University. It would mean a return to commuting to shows, and also commuting to school, making an hour-and-fifteen-minute drive from the Cape to Providence twice a week.

It was a time of frustration, a time many riders, especially those as young as Kate, might have done something drastic. Others might have gone in a grand prix completely overfaced and had troubles. Others might have taken over the riding duties of Sebastian, a legitimate grand prix horse. Others might even have said the hell with it and returned their focus to winning classes that were easier, just to win.

Kate did none of these. In her well-balanced way, she kept it all in perspective. No whining. No tantrum. No blaming the horses. She didn't like it, but she understood her situation and focused on trying to make it better.

*   *   *

Beezie and John didn't make the trip east. Instead, they went west to the Trader's Point Grand Prix in Indiana. It was a worthwhile trip. Beezie and Schnapps combined for their first grand prix victory as a pair.

Schnapps, a ten-year-old Thoroughbred, was one of the horses that had come to John Madden Sales after Florida, transferred there by owner Harry Gill from Michael's Vintage Farm. The horse had been on Australia's 1988 Olympic squad before coming to the U.S.

Earlier, Beezie and John had a busy show at the Oak Brook Jumper Classic. There, Mario Deslauriers, a Canadian riding under John's guidance, won the $40,000 Zurich-American Chicago Grand Prix on Roche. He also finished fifth as the fastest 4-faulter on Box Car Willie. Beezie and Schnapps had a double clear in the class, finishing third. Beezie also finished tied for seventh on Prost and on Grand Up. Also in the grand prix had been Hyun Jin Moon on French Rapture, and Un Jin Moon on The Girl Next Door. It was another typically busy horse show for Beezie and John.

That was the tenor of the summer. With Northern Magic on the sidelines recovering from the abscess, much of the focus was on others, on the clients. Work continued on preparing Un Jin and Hyun Jin Moon to ride for South Korea in the Barcelona Olympics. This was another show in the Midwest where several of their clients lived, another time of ten, twelve entries in each of the amateur classes.

*   *   *

Elsewhere in August, Goldstein and Saluut II continued their roll through the grand prix season, winning the $50,000 Continental Airlines Grand Prix at the Attitash Equine Festival. Norman Dello Joio and Amica, a gray Dutch-bred mare, won the $60,000 Crown Royal Grand Prix at Collingwood, Ontario. It was the third time within a little more than a month that the thirty-five-year-old Dello Joio, whose father had composed the Pulitzer Prize–winning *Meditations on Ecclesiastes*, had ridden to victory in a Canadian grand prix. Also, Buddy Brown and Charlebois won the International Jumping Derby in Stowe, Vermont. It was the fourth time the veteran rider had won the event.

*   *   *

Finally, nearly seven months after his arrest, one of two men arrested in connection with the death of a horse that was deliberately injured and had to be put down decided to change his plea. Harlow Arley voluntarily pleaded guilty to charges of animal cruelty and insurance fraud. Both were felonies. The change in his plea meant eighteen months in prison. The thirty-two-year-old Arley also agreed to testify against his co-defendant Tommy Burns, whose trial was set for mid-October.

CHAPTER 11

Little Lady
on a Big Roll

This was the closest to home turf that Beezie and John would know
during the grand prix season of 1991. Even if it was three hours from
home, New Hope Farm had become, while not a second home, at least
a second base from which to work. Tucked into the Neversink River
valley, this was where Un Jin and Hyun Jin Moon, children of the
controversial Rev. Sun Myung Moon, head of the Unification Church,
stabled their considerable string of horses. Because of this, Beezie and
John spent much of their time in the palatial barns and on the vast green
fields of what had become an equestrian showplace. The plan normally
called for them to drive the three hours from Cazenovia to Port Jervis, a
small town near where New York, New Jersey and Pennsylvania meet,
after working their horses in Cazenovia in the morning. Then they'd
work the horses at New Hope and stay the night. In the morning, they'd
reverse the process, working the Moons' horses after breakfast, driving
the backroads of the Catskill Mountains home to work their horses, sleep
and begin the process anew the next day. When they weren't at horse
shows, that was the drill.

Now they were at a show. The Autumn Classic, with its $100,000
Han Corporation Grand Prix, was in its third year at New Hope Farm.
Beyond being an impressive show with a lot of prize money, this was also

the place of a little extra pressure for Beezie and John. Un Jin and Hyun Jin Moon would ride in the grand prix in their home arena. Naturally, it was hoped they'd do well. This was just one more thing added to the already busy schedule of the team from John Madden Sales. It was a big thing at that, a little bigger this year as the two Moons were preparing for the Summer Games at the Olympics.

If that weren't enough, the Autumn Classic of 1991 was the site of the East Coast finals of the International Jumper Futurity. John, along with Linda Allen, had been the driving force behind this program and an incentive fund to encourage Americans to develop young horses for jumping. For too long the U.S. had relied on basically two sources for horses to go into the jumper ranks: rejects from the racetrack and Europe. Breeding Thoroughbreds to race was where the money had long been in the American horse industry. Breeding farms like Calumet and Claiborne farms produced dynasties and flourished. They flourished especially in the 1980s when Arab oil money seemed to flow in a pipeline from the Middle East to the big stud farms of Kentucky. This encouraged increased breedings, and not every one resulted in the new Northern Dancer or Seattle Slew. A surplus of horses grew, a boon to riders and trainers scouring the backsides of tracks for reasonably priced horses to convert to jumpers. The other source was Europe. The bottomless American checkbook became a staple of the 1980s for Europeans. Because of these things, there were but a handful of people making the sizable investment of time and money to build jumpers from the breeding shed up. John and Allen hoped the IJF would reverse that, making it more feasible for more people to breed for the show ring and not just for the track.

So it was with a full plate that the Autumn Classic opened in early September for Beezie and John. As it had the previous two years, the show opened amid comments about its being the "Moonie" show, and jokes about mass marriages. It also opened amid comments that it was one of the best of its kind in the country.

"I'd show here as often as they'd hold shows," said Tim Grubb. "The people are nice. The facilities are excellent. The prize money is great. The footing is terrific. Why not?"

About the only outward difference between this and any other show was that riders, grooms and spectators could quench their thirsts with a couple of different drinks. They could belly up to the concession stand and buy Ginseng Up or Mc Col, both soft drinks made in South Korea. Aside from that, it was little different from a show as American as Devon.

Like Devon, the Autumn Classic of 1991 offered spectators an outstanding grand prix.

After a parade of riders and a retirement ceremony for Forever, Michael walked the course with Ken Krause, who with Peter Doubleday was announcing the class. Using a remote microphone, Michael offered his observations on the course, one that beforehand he had described as being "Certainly big enough. But for $100,000 it should be."

Leslie Burr Lenehan, after walking the course, walked toward Jane Forbes Clark, eyes wide, arms outstretched, and said, "It's hooooge!"

Starting with the first ride, the large field of horses and riders were going to get a chance to see just how big and how demanding. That first ride was by Goldstein and Sebastian. Kate stood on a folding chair next to Patty Harnois on a raised portion of the area around the arena. From there she watched Goldstein ride Sebastian as if someone had suggested that she could ride no more after this particular round. In that round, the nine-year-old gray, Dutch-bred stallion looked as if he were auditioning for the role of Pegasus. He flew. With Goldstein appearing to push every right button in the right order, Kate's excitement grew as the pair cleared the fourteen-jump, seventeen-effort course that Richard Jeffrey had set.

Goldstein and Sebastian had served notice. They were clear and fast. If Jeffrey had set a course designed to make the riders earn the big prize money the old-fashioned way, Goldstein's round with Sebastian let them know they'd have to do it quickly as well. Time allowed was 95 seconds. Sebastian's time was 86.221. That's the way it should have been. There were fifty-four entries in the grand prix that Saturday evening in September, and the course would weed them out.

Kate and Harnois were ecstatic as they rushed down the steps to greet Goldstein in the warmup area. It was hard to imagine a better round than that. The next three rounds, all by top riders on experienced horses, proved that it would be no cakewalk in Port Jervis that night.

"That's all right, Gembo," Frank Chapot said as he patted Gem Twist after his round, the one immediately after Goldstein and Sebastian. Gem and Best had 8 faults. It was an off night for Gem Twist; he was flat.

Terry Rudd and P.S. Gazpacho had 4. Beezie and Schnapps were barely edged from the jump-off, taking 4 faults at the triple.

"He jumped frickin' unbelievable," said Grubb as he dropped off of Denizen, who had just posted the second clear of the night. This was just the latest in a string of such impressions made by the horse on the rider. Grubb had put together a group of people to buy the horse shortly after Eric Hasbrouck rode him to victory at the Children's Services Grand Prix in the spring. Grubb said he had people standing in line to buy a piece of this talented young horse. "He was well over everything out there. Room to spare."

Box Car Willie and Mario Deslauriers then posted a clear of their own. After that, Jeffrey's course began to claim its victims: Debbie Shaffner and Texas T, Stacy Cascio and Boss & Company, young David Olynick and Big Time, Michael Dorman and Olisco, Ray Texel and Ike, Buddy Brown and Charlebois, Henri Prudent and Reveur, Beezie and Sunset, George Lindemann, Jr., and Playback, Michael and Manassas County, Jeffrey Welles and Serengeti.

It wasn't until Andre Dignelli and Gaelic that there was another clear round.

If the course took its toll on the horses, it did so too on at least one rider. Christian Currey and Gentleman Jack Mirador had an outstanding round in the works. They were clear, and the young Tennesseean, sponsored of late by the Jack Daniels distillery's Gentleman Jack premium bourbon, and the thirteen-year-old Selle Français had but two more fences to clear before joining the jump-off. Heading into the number 13 fence, Currey lost his balance and fell into the green-and-white oxer. It was nearly a duplication of a fall during a grand prix in Memphis, one in which he had broken several ribs, one of which punctured a lung.

By the time the crowd settled back into their seats, Currey was up, collecting his horse and adjusting the Neoprene brace he wore around his midsection. He and Mirador retired.

"Ring rust," he said afterwards. He had just returned from taking time off after the fall in Memphis and was still trying to get his form back.

Although he was unable to add his name to the jump-off list, seven other horse-rider combinations did. As expected, Lisa Jacquin and For The Moment had a first-round clear. So did Norman Dello Joio on Amica, and again on Irish. Darlene Sandlin and Alley Oop did too, continuing to cement their presence on the East Coast show-jumping scene in their first venture here from the Midwest.

Leslie Lenehan and Fortus also joined the jump-off in commanding fashion. As they rode out, Wendy Chapot was waiting in the warmup area with a bucket of Kentucky Fried Chicken—dinner. Michael, wandering through the warmup area as Leslie and Jane Forbes Clark ate, joked with them.

"Is that how you pay her?" he said to Clark. "Just make sure there's some left for the jump-off." Someone suggested that the chicken be placed behind the last jump-off fence, a variation of the carrot and stick.

Finally, riding next to last, fifty-two horses after she opened the night on Sebastian, Goldstein doubled her chances at winning the $30,000 first prize. Saluut II wasn't nearly as careful as was Sebastian, giving the Autumn Classic jump a mean rattle but getting a break and having it stay in its cups. Still, they were clean.

As the jump crew readied the ring for the jump-off, Best walked the course with Krause, offering some insight on what the ten horse-rider combinations would face as they raced for the money. The course explained, the strategy outlined, Best and Krause walked out of the ring as Goldstein and Sebastian walked in.

Deslauriers, Grubb and Jacquin were in a line at the gate as it swung shut. As they had in the first round, Goldstein and Sebastian were determined to set the time to beat. Even though she had another chance, a good one with Saluut II, Goldstein looked as though she was out to make it Kate's gray stallion that won. Sebastian probably would have if it hadn't been for the fence about halfway through the jump-off round. In a split-second lapse, Goldstein let Sebastian get his eye off the fence, and the vertical came down. That was their undoing. In the end, they finished with 11 jumping and 41 time faults. What started out as a possible wire-to-wire win became a low-ribbon performance.

"So much heart," Goldstein said to Kate. "He tried to make it. Really tried."

Grubb and Denizen took 4 faults.

So did Deslauriers and Box Car Willie. After they exited with 4 faults, John, Beezie and Terry Bradner joined him at the in-gate. They left, hurriedly collecting Deslaurier's wife as they did.

It was left to Dignelli and Gaelic to post the first jump-off round without a knockdown. They were clear in 40.064. Jacquin and For The Moment duplicated the effort, lowering the time to beat to 39.178. However, making the cut to the last fence, Jacquin gave herself a little extra room, not cutting it quite as close as she might have.

"You left the door open," Michael said to Jacquin when she exited the ring. "You just have to hope that no one gets in."

Lenehan and Fortus tried but couldn't: 12 faults. Dello Joio and Amica tried and couldn't: 9 jumping and 19 time faults. Sandlin and Alley Oop got a foot in that door but weren't quick enough to enter: no faults but a time of 40.311. Jacquin's lead stood.

As Sandlin walked out of the ring, Goldstein and Saluut II walked in.

She quickly confirmed the idea that just about everyone in the place had, the idea that she was not going to try to step through the open door, she was going to blast through it. There was no mistake at 8A as there had been with Sebastian. The pair raced through the course. At the Johnny Walker planks, Saluut II rattled the fence, but luck was riding with this pair that night; it stayed up. Applause erupted: 35.550.

Only Dello Joio and Irish could undo Goldstein's eighth grand prix win of the year. They couldn't: 4 jumping and 2 time faults.

Harnois, Margie, Kate and Spank converged in one embrace. Young girls with papers and pens in hand seemed to sprout from the ground and surround the winner.

Nearby, Jacquin stood alone, quiet and pensive in the scurry that is a horse show when the big class of the night is over and everyone has someplace else to be. She looked at the ground in the warmup area as if she might find an answer. For the second straight year, she had finished second at this $100,000 class. The year before it had been George Lindemann, Jr., and Threes & Sevens who edged her. This time it was the winningest rider on the grand prix circuit this season. The seesaw tipped back in Goldstein's favor.

In the end, a total of 4.753 seconds separated the top four finishers. A total of 3.620 of that amount was between Goldstein and Jacquin. It had been a class worth $100,000. Dignelli collected $13,000 of that for his double-clear third-place finish. Then came Sandlin and Alley Oop in only their third show since moving to the East Coast to train with Ronnie Beard.

"I'm competing with people—Joe Fargis and Leslie Lenehan and Lisa Jacquin—I grew up admiring," she said. "I guess I'm a little star-struck, and this was easily the most difficult class we've been in. I'm pleased he [Alley Oop] was up to it."

Sandlin was also impressed that she was riding with Margie Goldstein, who that night became the first American rider to win eight grand prix in one season, a record. Five of those were on the Johnny Walker AGA circuit, another record. It had already been an impressive year, and indoors was still a month off.

Not bad for a kid from Miami who mucked stalls for her first lessons and rode every cast-off, reject, awful horse that came her way when she started out. Not bad for a self-proclaimed "little Jewish girl with no money." Not bad at all. After a year of injury and disappointment, Goldstein had not made a mere comeback, she had exploded back into the forefront of American show jumping.

Getting there had been a difficult process, one Goldstein could not forget.

It began as a fourth-grader, visiting a barn with a friend. This was enough to fuel her love of animals in a new direction.

"Every stray dog or cat that came along, I adopted," she said. "I brought home baby rats and iguanas, and hatched baby ducks at home."

Shortly, Goldstein was spending more and more time around animals, working in the kennels of a local barn owned by Dorothy and Robert Kramer. In addition to the dogs and cats she tended, Goldstein became more and more fascinated with the horses and ponies at this boarding and lesson barn she rode the bus to and from each day.

At the time, Goldstein's parents simply didn't have the money for riding lessons and show expenses. They were putting Goldstein's two older brothers through college, and even the salaries of two profession-als—he a CPA and she a teacher—didn't have enough in them to support a riding habit. Fortunately, the Kramers were able to help out.

"I was lucky that they saw how much I wanted it," Goldstein said of the Kramers. "They were some of the nicest people in the world, and they needed someone to show their ponies. It was me."

Before long, Goldstein was not only riding their ponies but had quickly become one of the busiest child catch riders in Florida. Then, at the age of sixteen, the relationship between Goldstein and the Kramers, who by then had bought Goldstein her first saddle, changed. Dorothy Kramer died.

The next show season, Margie became a surrogate horse show mom for the Kramers' daughter. Bob Kramer gave Margie a truck, a horse trailer, two horses and a credit card so his daughter could continue showing while he stayed home and took care of the farm. Goldstein, just sixteen years old and the ink barely dry on her driver's license, traveled across the Florida circuit with Terri Kramer, then just twelve years old.

While there was no trust-fund money, there was Puck W. It was this 17.1-hand Dutch Warmblood that helped Goldstein get on the path to the kind of season 1991 turned out as. He was a moose in horse's clothing, a moose that had once got a bit headstrong, taken off and jumped the back of a flat-bed truck and the woman sitting on it. Goldstein also told of riding a Saddlebred in a jumping class, straining to see the jumps around the horse's head. Still, they were horses to ride.

Those beginnings have never ended for Goldstein. She hasn't forgotten everyone who was there, everyone who let her ride their horses—good, bad or otherwise—when she was getting started. That was apparent at a show near Miami in 1988. In one day, Goldstein rode sixty-three different horses. She rode so much in the one day of that show that she wore the skin off the inside of her legs. She didn't get rich off any of this. She rode for $10 or $15 per horse, helping out friends who had helped her out in the past, doing for others what someone else had done for her. It wasn't about the money, or about riding as often as possible. It was about putting back into the sport what she had been fortunate enough to take out. Goldstein is not one to forget.

That's what made the 1990 season that much more difficult. She had been riding Roman Delight in the jump-off of a preliminary class the first week of Tampa, when the horse slipped and fell. It was at that moment that the previous year's AGA Rider of the Year was to be sidelined for about ten weeks. In the fall, Roman Delight landed on her ankle. What resulted was not a fracture, not a break, not a strain or sprain. Goldstein had crushed most of the bones in the ankle.

Even after recovering and returning to the ring, Goldstein struggled. She had her boot altered, the back being slit and a zipper inserted so she could slide her foot in. It wouldn't bend. Much of that season she negotiated her way around showgrounds in a golf cart. She limped noticeably. Still, she couldn't not ride.

It was, at least in part, that amount of time she didn't ride, the classes she didn't win that helped make her so successful in 1991. The same could be said for the horses in her life. Goldstein, young and starting out, didn't have the money to buy fancy, made horses or the connections to get them.

*   *   *

Watching Sebastian be so close but not making it was about the way things had gone for her own riding. She hadn't ridden as well as she could have. Again, instead of being in the grand prix, Kate was watching, riding in the amateur classes but not riding the way she wanted to. At one point in the summer, she was feeling that with a break here and there, an outside chance existed that she would be in the parade of riders before the grand prix at Port Jervis.

"I felt like I could have done better," she said. "I guess I still had Southampton in my mind and was really wanting to do better."

As much as she thrilled at watching Sebastian do so well in the grand prix, it was difficult for Kate to not want to be the rider. He had fully recovered from the back injury he sustained in Florida, and had regained his form and confidence.

"I have everything I can do to keep believing that this was the best thing to do for him, to wait," she said. "I just keep thinking how it's going to be really great when I get on him and ride in the grand prix. It would be silly for me to get on him now when he's doing so well in the grand prix just for myself."

She thought about doing a small grand prix after New York, riding the horse she owned but wasn't competing on. That thought was fleeting. She continued putting the horses before herself.

Thus far the year had been a drastic departure from just about all of Kate's riding up until this year.

"I won ribbons, good ones, in the amateur classes last year," she said. "I try not to get down. This far into the year, the worst thing I could do is get depressed. But I'd still like to be putting in a few more clean rounds. Sometimes I catch myself thinking about the grand prix, I don't care if it's big or harder for me to ride, I just wish I could do it.

"This is a lesson: you didn't do the grand prix here, you didn't do well in the amateurs, you've had a year to try to do it and that should tell you something, forget it. It's September again. I know I can do it. Suddenly I felt like I had all this time and I can't do it. No, the horses may not be the ideal match-up for me, but I should be able to ride them around a grand prix. I hate blaming the horses.

"I just keep thinking: Florida, Florida, Florida."

*   *   *

When the grand prix riders reappeared in the ring to collect their ribbons, one was missing. Deslauriers and Box Car Willie were not there for the ceremony.

The young Canadian had rushed to the hospital where two of his grooms had been taken. On their way to the class that night, the car they were in left the twisting road near New Hope Farm and crashed. Badly. It flipped several times.

Rumors spread quickly: one was dead; both were.

As the night wore on the accident became the topic of conversation at many stalls where horses were being put up for the night and tack cleaned and rides critiqued.

It was at the stalls of Vintage Farm. Other accidents were recounted, including one about a groom who was in a head-on collision during Southampton.

"Now, everyone, drive carefully," Michael said as he left his grooms to finish the conversation. Walking away he said, "It makes you wonder.

I just saw her walking her puppy this morning. You think, I had eight faults. Big deal."

The next day, the rumors were set aside. It had been an accident all right, but neither woman was killed. Injured badly, yes, but not killed.

After Port Jervis, Michael had 4 faults on Manassas County and 8 on Heisman at the $75,000 Cadillac American Gold Cup. Then the other kind of Thoroughbreds in Michael's life would get his attention. He and D. D. attended the sales in Lexington. He did some clinics. Then he was off to ride for the Team in Mexico, a place with strong memories for him, a foreign show he liked to attend.

*   *   *

The year before, late September meant the East Coast show-jumping community ventured to Baltimore for a taste of indoors before the major shows of the fall. Not so in 1991. Baltimore had folded, leaving behind some disappointed riders who liked the show.

Instead, they convened in upstate New York's Genesee Valley at the Rochester Classic. While it wasn't Baltimore, it still was a World Cup qualifier, and that alone attracted riders who otherwise might not have shown. It also attracted a considerable amount of grumbling. The stabling. The footing. The basics were not up to snuff. Besides, it was cold. It was mid-September and it felt like January. Temperatures dropped into the teens, and while the classes were in the Dome Center at the fairgrounds in suburban Henrietta, schooling and stabling were outdoors. Temperatures had dropped so drastically that some horses began to grow their thicker winter coats, and the favorite vendor at the show turned out to be a young entrepreneur who was selling hand-knit sweaters imported from Ecuador.

The grumbling reached a peak in the qualifying class for the grand prix. During this class, Goldstein refused to jump. Instead she entered the ring and rode through the timers. The footing was so bad that she didn't want the horses to have to thunder down onto it any more than they absolutely had to. Still, she and everyone else in the qualifier made it into the grand prix.

For Beezie, riding in the cozy confines of the Dome Center had proven beneficial in the past. She had won the grand prix the first two years of the Classic, 1989 and 1990. Paired with Schnapps, it looked like she might maintain ownership of the title.

Nine riders made it to the jump-off, clearing Frank Chapot's twisty course without fault. The final round then began to take its toll: James

Young, 17 faults; Barney Ward, 8. Five riders ended with 4 faults. One of that number was the rider with the fastest time of the round.

Beezie and Schnapps looked confident as they entered the ring. With each jump, more of the crowd got behind their efforts. They were aware of her shot at the "three-peat," and also appreciated the speed with which the pair cruised the course. The small arena reverberated as Beezie and Schnapps bore down on the final jump, a massive oxer. The victory was theirs until Schnapps's front feet grazed the back rail of the fence. It toppled. So did the cheers of the crowd.

"What a shame," said John. "What a shame."

It was the third time in a jump-off that Schnapps had taken out the final fence.

In the end, Buddy Brown and Charlebois won. They were just fast enough and careful enough to edge George Lindemann, Jr., and Playback by a little less than a second.

Afterward, Brown uncorked and passed around the Baccarat crystal decanter of Johnny Walker that, like a new saddle, was part of the win. He toasted Charlie Boy, his name for the Thoroughbred he said reminded him of Sugar Ray, one of his most successful mounts.

Three American teams spread out to represent the USET in international competition in September. The lone victory occurred during Rochester when the Team won at Lanaken, Belgium. It was there that Shaffner, Best, Lenehan and Scharffenberger won. The victory was announced during the Rochester Classic, almost as a bulletin of importance. It was tinged with a bit of extra drama as Brian Flynn announced that "our countrymen," making the Team sound more like combat heroes than equestrians, had won in Belgium. There was mild cheering, but for some it was a feeling of "Finally!" that overcame them. It had seemed that maybe Katie Monahan Prudent had been right—or at least struck a nerve—when she wrote an article for *U.S. Horse World* that carried the threatening headline: "We May Never Win Again," and spoke of America's fall from show-jumping greatness and how it was linked to the Dolan lawsuit.

However, that European trip of late summer created something more than a much-needed international win. Especially at Lanaken, the Americans were a team in spirit as well as in name. The Team members went places together, they ate meals together, they schooled together. There were not four individuals at the show who happened to be from the U.S. Instead, there was a team.

Part of the reason was the emergence of Steve Stephens as the chef d'equipe for the European swing. It was a role he relished, one into which he threw himself.

Stephens had apprenticed himself to Frank Chapot during the Pan American Games. He also endeared himself to every American with the USET on that trip when he made a mad dash to a K mart to buy six toilet seats to take to Havana. The toilets, even in the athletes' village, were *sans* seats.

In Europe, Stephens went beyond mere sanitary comfort for the American riders. He tried to emulate the style of Bert deNemethy, the man most people credit with creating the dynasty which American show jumping began. Trained in the Hungarian cavalry school, deNemethy made things happen, he made things work, he improved riders and horses. It was his attention to detail that made the USET a winning squad.

Each day, Stephens worked with riders, attended to details, made sure the grooms had transportation and imbued the outing at Lanaken with deNemethy-style team spirit. Every day the drawling Floridian faxed reports home.

In the end, the USET won an international competition. To be sure, the Lanaken squad was one of experience, both in horses and riders. But Stephens added to the mix, worked to make it happen, worked to make it a team. In the end, the likes of Volan and Gem Twist aside, Stephens's efforts counted for something toward that victory.

*　　　*　　　*

Kate had done better at the Gold Cup, taking three rails in the qualifier for the grand prix that was won by Terry Rudd. She did okay at Rochester. Still, this did little to set aside her uneasiness.

"Now I know so many more people at the show," she said. "They're nice and say, 'Don't worry, you'll get there,' and I feel like saying, 'Well, I've won classes!' It gets frustrating when they associate you with going and never getting a ribbon. I hadn't realized until now how I had gotten used to people saying, 'Oh, you're Kate Chope. I saw you win . . .' "

Still there was no thought of doing the grand prix at smaller shows, stepping down a level and giving herself an opportunity to win a class.

"I just love the big shows and I don't like the feeling of having to go to a smaller show in order to do better."

CHAPTER 12

Indoors: The Third Season

Maury McGrath sat in the stabling office of the Pennsylvania National Horse Show doing needlepoint. The normal craziness of his job had temporarily abated. It was not by design, though, that he was creating a Dalmatian in thread.

McGrath, who in his spare time hand-crafts wooden tack trunks, was idled due to technical difficulties. Severe technical difficulties. It seems that someone had spilled a cup of coffee into the keyboard of his computer, the machine that keeps all of his stabling assignments, as well as Tetrus, the video game he played in moments of relative calm on his job. Computer keyboards have become disposable items, easily replaced. Not so easily replaced are some of the inner workings of the machine, which shorted out as the keyboard went through its death throes.

Indoors had gotten off to a rocky start for McGrath.

It was October. More importantly, it was a season apart from the rest of the year. "Florida" is not just a state in which to show jumpers. It is a state of mind, a season unto itself, a time bracketed by December and April and prompting a certain routine, an outlook separate from the remainder of the year. "Indoors" is like that too. To these people it is not a location. Instead it is a series of three or four shows that to many is the reason they do the rest, the reason there is a "Florida" and all of those shows between it and "indoors."

Indoors: Harrisburg, Washington, the National. Add Toronto to the list of some. Those shows, especially the three in the U.S., are different from anything that occurs in the previous nine months. These are the black-tie shows, society events that wheel around horses. They are shows with history, ones about which everyone has a story, a memory. Ones that seem to be adored by amateurs, and tolerated by many of the professionals.

To be sure, there are other shows held indoors. Port Jervis. Rochester. These are not part of indoors. They are simply shows that happen to be held inside. Harrisburg, Washington and the National have the flavor and flair of an international show, the Canadians, the French, the British being there. Usually these shows offer the only opportunities Americans have to see the stars of international teams compete. Plus, these are the shows that have different classes, ones that help define their specialness. These are the shows of the puissance and the relays, the match races, ones that make the pulse of the spectator quicken. These too are the shows of pageantry. Harrisburg featured a military school marching band. On the schedule for the National was the band from the Merchant Marine Academy. Indoors is also a time for the spectators, even the ones who barely know one end of the horse from the other, and these people have to be entertained. Still, the centerpiece of these shows, hoopla and other horse breeds aside, had to be the open jumpers, and especially the grand prix.

There is another side to indoors, one not so glamorous. These three major shows come at the end of the long season. It's as much the sound horse as the great one that stays healthy in these days of almost continuous showing. Indoors then becomes a test of strategy, one of pacing. Horses must be kept sound, but still show often enough to please the owners, to earn money, to stay near the eye of the sport, and now to retain their spots on the IBM/USET computer list. Indoors then becomes the last battle in a year-long war of attrition.

All of that makes indoors hard on a horse like Lisa Jacquin's For The Moment. As Harrisburg rolled around, he was near the top of the computer list, he was in the running for AGA Horse of the Year honors and he was the only horse with which Jacquin could really campaign. For the older horse, even one as fit and sturdy and reliable as For The Moment, indoors could be arduous.

Those three big shows at the end of the season have the same impact on people as well. By this time, riders and grooms and barn managers are tired, worn thin after the demands of living on the road. The schedules for indoors are anything but leisurely, and stabling anything but convenient. Besides, this community on wheels has lived together almost since breaking camp after Florida, and some nerves have been rubbed raw. And there is a bottom line to indoors, a hefty one: such shows are expensive.

Nevertheless, indoors remained a draw for many riders.

Kate was one such rider. She liked indoors, felt invigorated by it, she built toward it.

On a warm, sunny day toward the end of Harrisburg, Kate took Ginsing out for a hack away from the business and deep footing of the schooling ring next to the State Farm Show Arena. The pair stepped gingerly across the massive asphalt parking lot before reaching the narrow band of grass between it and the highway. She walked him at first, then began an easy trot toward a large spot of grass at the far end of the parking lot. Once there, she worked the edges, staying close to the perimeter, avoiding the darkened middle, which had, after some rain and a number of other horses, become slick.

Making a circle around the green expanse, Kate would move Ginsing into a canter, one that easily consumed distance in three-beat bites. She smiled as she rode, chin raised and facing into the morning sun. That morning, Kate rode in the elemental way of someone as at ease with the movement of the horse as she was with her own walking. Small and slight, Kate became of the horse, not on it, and this is what separates horsemen from people who ride horses. It was a time to see why she had shown up at Holly Hill as a child in a shirt with horses on it, and never really left. As she hacked the horse in the sun, away from the pageantry and the cheering crowds and the flower-bedecked jumps, Kate and Ginsing illustrated the bond between all true riders and their horses. She was the best of riding, Ginsing the best of everything that began with eohippus. They could not have been farther from team selection lawsuits, insurance fraud trials, sponsorships and brightly colored horse-show ribbons had they been on the steppes of Asia.

"This is where you get to know the horse," she said. "This is fun."

That spirit was reflected in the way she rode in the ring. As indoors began, Kate had captured the smoothness over which she had agonized at Southampton, Port Jervis and Rochester. The rhythm was there. So was the confidence. Even arriving at the show late because of her genetics class at Brown and having to fly back to take a test, Kate rode strongly.

There was confidence in her movements, the kind she developed riding Hearsay, steady old Henry, in amateur classes and being in the ribbons almost all the time.

Kate was one of twenty-eight entries in the $50,000 Michelob Grand Prix De Penn National, the first of the major events of indoors. As the year-ending shows do, this grand prix attracted many of the top riders with their top horses: Michael Dorman and Olisco, Anne Kursinski and Starman, Joe Fargis and Mill Pearl, Lisa Jacquin and For The Moment, Margie Goldstein and Saluut II, Debbie Shaffner and Volan. Like the other shows of indoors, Harrisburg was also a lure to riders from the West and Midwest. Mike McCormick from Flower Mound, Texas, and Peter Pletcher of Magnolia, Texas, were there. So were Philip Cillis and Juniperus from Encinitas, California.

Linda Allen set the course. As Rich and Shelly Fellers walked it, they had company. Harrisburg marked the debut of their son Christopher, just a month after he was born while his father was showing at Spruce Meadows. As the couple walked the grand prix course, Christopher rode in the comfort of a pack strapped across the front of his mother. He remained snug there later while Shelly braided the mane of Kourous, the horse Rich was riding.

"He'll either love horses or hate them," she said of her son. Christopher had made the Pan Am trip, waiting to be born just weeks after his parents arrived back in the U.S. Shelly had taken a break from grooming while Rich continued on to Spruce Meadows. Harrisburg marked her first show back. She'd consult with her husband about a fence, then, as she counted strides to the next fence, she would look down and smile at Christopher.

Adam Prudent accompanied his mother and father, Katie Monahan Prudent and Henri Prudent, around the course. He sat atop a wall jump waving his arms, laughing with his mother, who was preparing to ride Silver Skates, the surprise of her grand prix season.

The other side of the course, leaning against a fence, his head resting in his hand, elbow propped against the top rail, McLain Ward surveyed the task ahead. Ward was closer in age to Adam Prudent than he was to the child's mother. Still, he rode in the grand prix, the youngest rider ever to cash a winner's check in such an event. It was just days before the grand prix that Ward turned sixteen ("Finally!" he announced). It was just the latest of birthdays celebrated at this show, and one like the many that would come ("I know where I'll spend my birthday for the next thirty or forty years"). It was reassuring to hear Ward, among the brightest of the new stars on the American grand prix scene, sound like a sixteen-year-old. To see him around the shows, Ward was a man, reserved, proper, businesslike. Often, he competed with men and women twice his age, almost always without belying his own, riding in major grand prix with the skill and courage of an adult.

Allen's course sorted out who'd make it to the jump-off.

Kate and Ginsing, riding near the middle of the pack, took 19 jumping faults and a slew of time faults. Odd as it may seem, it still was a good ride. It was nowhere near the ribbons, but still Kate rode smoothly, she rode confidently. It was October and indoors, and Kate rode Ginsing as if Southampton and Port Jervis hadn't happened.

Beezie and Schnapps were also eliminated from the ribbon race.

Only five riders made it to the seven-effort jump-off of this World Cup qualifier and only three of those went clear.

Goldstein and Saluut II had 4 faults.

Kursinski and Starman went next: clear in 31.501.

Next was David Raposa and Seven Wonder. They upset the Michelob planks for 4 faults.

Fargis and Mill Pearl went clear and less than a second behind Kursinski, with a time of 32.378.

Shaffner and Volan took the last shot at the course and at catching Kursinski and Starman. Harrisburg was another time for Shaffner to do what she does as well as any American grand prix rider, act as an ambassador of the sport. *Horseplay* had just come out with the second in a series of posters. This one features Shaffner and Volan clearing a fence. Part of the proceeds from the sale of the poster benefit the USET, just like an earlier one of Greg Best and Gem Twist.

Shaffner signed posters, personalizing them for anyone who asked. More than that, she talked to the people who stopped. She asked about their horses, about their riding. She answered questions and told youngsters about her horses. Shaffner sold show jumping to those who stopped by the autograph booth, instead of selling her autograph like some baseball players do.

In the ring, Shaffner and Volan, her poster mate, were clear. Their time was 32.330, good enough to finish ahead of Fargis, but not fast enough to unseat Kursinski.

"He was a good boy tonight, wasn't he?" said Kursinski afterward. Starman won the open jumper championship.

Indoors was under way in earnest.

*   *   *

For many, the next stop was Washington, D.C. Actually, it was Lan-dover, Maryland, site of the Capital Center, the arena that is to the Beltway what the Meadowlands is to Manhattan. This is the suburban sports palace for a nearby major city, the building that wouldn't attract as many events or as many spectators if it were inside that same city.

It was here that Darlene Sandlin made her debut for the USET. She had hoped it would be memorable, and it was . . . for all the wrong reasons.

It was here that the fledgling National Grand Prix ended its first season with its Super Prix won by a journeyman Texan.

It was here that Goldstein almost earned another spot in the record books.

Sandlin is a testament to the success—at least for her—of the IBM/USET computer ranking system. That is what placed her on the Team.

"After all the negative and positive things that were said about the computer rankings, there's no way I could have made it on the Team without it," she said. "Obviously, I wanted to be at the top of the list, but I didn't go to every horse show thinking that if I win it I'd move up. It wasn't until after I went to ride with Ronnie [Beard] that I knew I was near the top of the list and might be asked to ride Washington. I couldn't believe it."

It was during the Gold Cup at Devon that Sandlin learned that dreams do come true. Beard had told her that Sally Ike, vice-president for show jumping for the USET, wanted to see her.

"She asked me in person and I was speechless. I had a refusal in the Gold Cup class and they still wanted me after that? It made my day, I'll say that. I was fairly depressed. I had not done well at the Gold Cup, and that really turned it around immediately."

But it really didn't sink in until she arrived at the Capital Center and was a Team rider and not an individual.

"It sank in pretty well when I went in the first class and was so amazingly nervous. I didn't want to make a fool of myself. I wanted to have my teammates proud of me. I put a lot of pressure on myself. I'm pretty good at that anyway. I didn't want to make a mistake. The hoopla about the computer ranking and whether I even belong there went through my mind."

Then it came time to prove herself.

"I galloped into the ring of my first class and fell off. I did everything I didn't want to do and got it out of my system. I didn't want to make a fool of myself. I wanted to do well for the Team. I *didn't* want to fall off. Not only did I fall off, but I broke the bridle. I couldn't even get back on. I crashed through the brick wall. A spectacle. My family had come to see me. My boyfriend had come to see me and give me support, and there I was lying in the dirt. It broke the tension."

After her debut, Sandlin was still well received. Others told her of other problems of other riders.

"It was nice to know I wasn't the first fool."

In the end, Washington was good for Sandlin. The show is one of the few that has a costume class for the international riders, a skit, the kind that enlivens especially the British shows. Before it, Sandlin and her boyfriend, Goldstein, Shaffner, Dorman and Beard went costume shopping. The excursion was a team effort, one that included Sandlin, elevating her as much as it brought her views of the other veteran riders down to earth.

In the Nations Cup she had 8 faults—faults she was quick to point out—in the first round. In the second round Ally Oop had a plank down. In the grand prix, Sandlin looked to be headed for a major victory when "It was like demons took over my body," she deadpanned, "And I just blew it at one jump and the rest of the course was just fine." She tied for second in the grand prix with the other 4-faulters.

In the end, Sandlin was pleased to have been a rookie on a Team that won the team title and was second in the Nations Cup.

Peter Pletcher won that grand prix, the President's Cup. For the thirty-one-year-old Texan and the ten-year-old Thoroughbred gelding Uncle Sam, it was the biggest win of the year. More than that, it was a validation of sorts for Texas show jumping in general. It wasn't the typical indoors scenario of the big-name American horse and rider walking off with the grand prix, or even someone from an international team taking the top prize. Pletcher, who started riding in a western saddle, was a Texan who beat out the easterners, one that many of his fellow riders were happy for.

Pletcher's win was the first of its kind. The National Grand Prix League, the competitor of the AGA, had wanted it to be viewed as the Super Bowl of American show jumping. Three riders from each "conference" had qualified and were the only riders eligible for the $20,000 in added awards. In addition to Pletcher, the West was represented by Tony Font and Mike McCormick, three Texans. Goldstein,

Fargis and Mario Deslauriers, as well as Tim Grubb, represented the East. Chris Kappler, Richard Cheska and Laura Kent Kraut were the three from the Midwest.

Furthermore, Pletcher was there only through the graces of the new league. He had not otherwise qualified, but his standing within the league made him one of three to represent the West. In addition to the grand prix prize money, Pletcher walked off with a cash bonus from the league, a new Rolex and a bronze sculpture.

The year 1991 had been good for the NGL, an attempt to create another vehicle other than the AGA. From all indications it worked. Mike Parrish, one of those involved in its formation, said the NGL met all of its orginal objectives, chief of which was helping shows become better at marketing the sport. The NGL also didn't lose money. Even in a bad economy, the new venture prospered.

CHAPTER 13
A Star Is Born

Paul Greenwood did something that a year before had been nearly impossible: the man laughed. He was all smiles and handshakes and hellos as he strolled through the hallway under the stands of the Brendan Byrne Arena at the Meadowlands in East Rutherford, New Jersey.

A year before he had paced the area that housed the offices of the management of the National Horse Show. He had been in charge of the show in 1990, the captain transferred to a ship already taking on water and listing badly, a ship he left before it had finished its painful, limping voyage.

In 1990 members of the management committee steeped in the tradition of the 107-year-old show grumbled that Greenwood dressed too casually, appearing not in tuxedo or hunt club pinks but in a suit and bow tie. No one said anything about Greenwood's attire in 1991 as he wandered through the show in boat shoes, corduroy jeans and a red sweater, his new wife by his side and the two of them laughing. He was just another exhibitor, there to watch from the grandstands as his horses performed. Greenwood had no worries about budgets, or concerns about snipers wearing National Horse Show badges. Neither did he have to cringe when he opened the *New York Times* in the morning.

It was a different Paul Greenwood at the 108th annual National Horse

Show, which opened to weather better suited to the likings of managers of outdoor shows.

Likewise, it was a different National Horse Show that he and other exhibitors and spectators attended. If Greenwood had captained a Titanic of a show, then the National of 1991 was a festive cruise ship filled with celebrating honeymooners.

The captain of this new ship was Sallie Wheeler. She occupied the dressing-room-turned-office Greenwood had occupied just a year before. The daughter of August Busch, she was as ebullient as Greenwood had been sullen when he sat in that same office. She was as openly optimistic as Greenwood had been guarded.

She could afford to be these things and more. Literally, she could afford to.

In 1990, Greenwood had tried, in effect, to run a massive four-stack ocean liner with a rowboat budget. Wheeler, on the other hand, had what some imagined to be a bottomless checkbook. She also had the cooperation and assistance of the Meadowlands, which embraced the show as a partner, as a first mate, and not just as a landlord, as it had a year earlier. These things combined to create a show of amenities, a horse show of goodwill, a horse show with a promotion budget.

Wheeler hadn't reclaimed the glory of the National when it was held at Madison Square Garden. Instead, she had created a new reality for the show, one of celebrities, one of spectators in the seats, one with a festive atmosphere. It didn't herald the arrival of Manhattan's social season, but the National Horse Show of 1991 was at least once again deserving of its name.

To do this, it cost about $2.5 million.

The National Horse Show, in addition to having Marty Bauman handle public relations, hired Joey Goldstein, a publicist, an old-time greaser of editorial wheels at newspapers, magazines and TV stations. The board hired a photographer equipped with a Leafax to transmit photos from the show directly to the wire services and daily newspapers. After each day of the show, videotaped highlights were sent to each New York City television station. The show was advertised in magazines, splashing a new full-color logo across the pages of equine magazines. In all, the National Horse Show increased spending back to the level of 1989 to bring people to the Meadowlands to watch the hunters and jumpers and Saddlebreds and coaching horses. In the austere year of 1990, the promotion budget was $100,000, down from $270,000 the previous year. Headlines in the *Times* and in the Newark *Star-Ledger* sang the praises of glitz and glamour and the National Horse Show. Even *Sports Illustrated* was there, reporter John Scher following Margie Goldstein for a feature on the winningest rider of the year. And NBC was there, doing research for the 1992 Olympics. In a media town, the media were at the National Horse Show.

The board also decided to give spectators more than just a horse show. They gave them entertainment. There was a petting zoo for children, pony rides, a carousel, educational displays, all free and all sponsored by companies like Coca-Cola, Carvel and Oscar Mayer, which even parked its famed Weinermobile at the show. The National of 1991 opened as the lights dimmed on Tuesday night and country-and-western singer Ronnie Milsap performed a short concert before the first class began. He played again at the close of the evening, and the opening-night faithful adjourned to a gala party in the Sheraton ballroom.

During the course of its six-day run, the National Horse Show also presented cutting-horse demonstrations by super model Christie Brinkley and Christina Paine, a paraplegic actress. John Payne, better known as the One-Armed Bandit, a one-armed cowboy herding long-horned cattle onto the roof of his specially-built stock trailer, also performed. Gaps between classes were filled by Lecile Harris, rodeo clown, and several times during the show the Svennsens, a trick-riding comedy team from Sweden, stood on and fell off a pair of horses to the delight of the crowd. Not surprisingly, the Budweiser Clydesdales also filled the arena, as special guests.

As a show with its base in New York City should, the National also had celebrities. Singer-songwriter Billy Joel watched his wife Christie Brinkley ride, actress Jane Russell appeared in the National's spotlight, and "Good Morning America" host and horsewoman Joan Lunden presented ribbons in a lead-line class. Show directors were able to don their ball gowns and pinks for a private dinner with Marilyn Quayle, the Vice President's wife, who then attended the show with Secret Service agents, in white tie, in tow.

Sallie Wheeler had become Flo Ziegfeld. The National Horse Show had become her Broadway.

But not everything was aimed at upping the glitz and glamour index of the National. There were other things, smaller ones, things that made the place just nicer to be at. Exhibitors could have free coffee and donuts in the mornings. Participants could have limousines, travel arrangements, show tickets, dinner reservations, and other matters handled by a concierge at the show. The ramp between the outdoor stabling and the arena was swept. Tony Hitchcock was hired as producer of the show, and his production meetings every morning at eleven made the show run on time.

Pony classes, after a twenty-three-year absence, were back. Not back, however, were the evening clothes the men of the board had previously worn all day, every day of the show. Instead, they wore modest blue blazers and gray slacks.

The National Horse Show wasn't back at the Garden, but it seemed to be back, if only from the edge of the grave. And it wasn't, for many, just another suburban horse show.

In many ways, the competition couldn't have been better had Hitchcock been allowed to orchestrate it during his morning production meetings. Recognizable names won major classes. A nice guy finished first. The National of 1991 was also the show where a new name joined the A-list of American show jumpers.

And there was a bit of tension, a ripple on the otherwise placid surface of the show. Even this was resolved without much trouble, an insight into the changing nature of show jumping as it wrestled to find its place in the larger arena of entertainment/sports.

On Wednesday night, the second evening of the show, one of the highlights of the show got under way. Seven horse-rider combinations had entered the puissance, the exciting test of a horse's ability to clear wide and high jumps as well as a test of the courage of both horse and rider.

The puissance this night would also test the patience of the show managers.

After three rounds, two riders were left: Margie Goldstein on Daydream and Joe Turi on Ever If Ever. All seven riders had been clear in the first round, the wall at 6'. Goldstein's other horse, Aristo, bowed out at 6' 5"; so did Leslie Lenehan on Ricarda, and Barney Ward on J.R. Number One. Texan Mike McCormick and Nessus II withdrew. Ian Millar and Czar made it one more round, faulting in the second round when the spread was 6' 6 " and the wall at 6' 11".

In the third jump-off the wall was at 7' 2".

Before what would have been the final round, Goldstein and Turi approached Jarrett Garner, gatekeeper and the link between management and the riders. They told him they would be just as happy to leave the competition as a tie . . . unless more money was offered to continue. That was the message a somewhat bemused Garner relayed by walkie-talkie to Peter Doubleday and David Distler.

Silence filled the arena. No attempt was made to fill the gap in activities as Goldstein and Turi negotiated with show managers. No rodeo clown, no celebrity, no long-horned cattle on top of horse trailers, no Michael Carney society orchestra playing.

The riders rightfully claimed the horses were tired, having jumped high and long just four days earlier at Washington. Besides, the management at Washington last week had offered Goldstein $10,000 to take a shot at the world puissance record, 7' 9". That alone equaled the entire purse for the event now hung up in negotiation by walkie-talkie.

"This is really hard on the horse," said Goldstein. "It takes a lot out of him. It's difficult to expect him to do it again, just after Washington. There should be an incentive for that."

Barney Ward took a shot at being the elder statesman, talking to Goldstein and Turi. Ian Millar announced to no one in particular that you don't change the rules in the middle of the competition. Neither ambassador succeeded.

Finally, Distler arrived at the somewhat edgy scene at the in-gate. He asked Nancy Jaffer of the Newark *Star-Ledger* and another reporter talking with Goldstein and Turi to leave, and they huddled.

Still, no sound, no Svennsens, no music, not even the pronouncement of technical difficulties.

In the end Goldstein and Turi agreed to continue the competition on the condition that the question of money would be resolved after the arena was cleared and the crowd had gone home. Both faulted at 7' 2". Tied.

The next day's Newark *Star-Ledger* sports pages carried a story by Jaffer discussing the puissance tempest in the horse show's teapot. It was received about the way Robin Finn's "obituary" in the *Times* had been exactly a year before. Jaffer's story did not, however, cast a pall over the rest of the show the way Finn's had. Things moved on, and the moment's bad press was soon swept away by other things.

"By the next day, all was forgotten," says Goldstein.

Henri Prudent won the $25,000 Cellular One and Metro Mobile World Cup Grand Prix on a horse named Trick Or Treat. Prudent's standby. The King, had been sold, and the new horse was supposed to be Alison Firestone's junior jumper horse. Instead it won the grand prix for the congenial thirty-six-year-old Frenchman, a favorite among other riders and show jumping's fans.

Another perennial good guy won the $100,000 Mercedes-Benz Grand Prix of New York. Jeffrey Welles won only one grand prix in 1991. He and Serengeti had saved the right performance for the right night. They were fast and accurate, winning $30,000 of the $100,000 offered in the timed first jump-off.

For Welles, the victory hardly seemed to ripple his smiling stoicism.

"My horse happened to be on tonight, and I was lucky enough for everything to work out," said Welles. "It happened to be her night."

It was the biggest win for the twenty-nine-year-old North Carolina native, paired with the eleven-year-old German-bred Holsteiner mare, which he and Jimmy Keyes had found through Astrid Winkler during a European buying trip. Welles, riding since the age of six, nursed the 16.2-hand gray mare through the preliminary jumper ranks until the horse was purchased by Frank and Karen Lloyd of Mahwah, New Jersey.

Clearly not as big as the win by Welles and Serengeti, and not tinged with sentimentality as the one by Prudent and Trick Or Treat, but the double clear by Darlene Sandlin and Alley Oop in the Nations Cup was one of the delights of the show, adding a bit of the Cinderella story to a show striving for memorable moments. In her first trip to the East Coast indoor season with an open jumper, the twenty-seven-year-old native of Kansas City surprised even herself.

She and Alley Oop had an impressive double fault-free go in the Nations Cup competition. Riding with Goldstein, Joe Fargis and Anne Kursinski, riders she has looked up to for years, Sandlin was in the middle of the Meadowlands arena as "The Star-Spangled Banner" was played at the end of the Nations Cup awards ceremony, and her face filled the Matrix, the larger-than-life, multiscreened television on the scoreboard. Tears flowed; Sandlin was swept up in the emotion of the moment.

Sitting atop Alley Oop, clearly her best friend, a lavish bouquet of flowers in her arms, her sandy hair and broad smile in stark counterpoint to her black velvet helmet and the red coat of the USET, Sandlin was living a dream, and unafraid to show how good it all felt.

Those were tears of joy, exhilaration. On past nights, not on horseback, not at center stage, not on the Matrix of the Meadowlands for the world to see, Sandlin had cried for other reasons. As a teenager, she lost first her mother, then her father to alcoholism. Then she married young. She tried to live without horses and found she couldn't. She divorced at an age when most women are just beginning to think about engagement rings.

Still, Sandlin had the smile of someone half her age and the insight, the wisdom, of a woman twice her twenty-seven years. All of her victories were hard won.

Like Welles, she was six when the first pony, a Shetland, arrived at her house in the country with a barn in the backyard. Then came a half-Arab, half–Quarter Horse pony, about the same age as Sandlin and still teaching her nieces how to ride.

"I have a fairly vivid memory of learning how to canter and being run away with," said Sandlin. "It was quite exciting. My mother had set up some tire jumps. The pony took off at full speed, jumped all those tire jumps and headed straight for the barn, and I loved every second of it. I thought that's what it was all about, the running, the jumping. Away we went. I thought it was great."

Sandlin used that pony for bareback barrel racing, riding through the back fields of the family farm, and showing. "Just about anything I could get into," she recalls.

The Sandlin horses and Darlene and two sisters outgrew the backyard, and in short order the family built a boarding and training stable.

"I remember the question was whether we should build a swimming pool or a barn, and the vote was for the barn," said Sandlin.

White Fox Manor is still operating near Kansas City. But it left the family some years ago.

Darlene's parents divorced when she was about ten years old. Her mother died when she was fourteen. Her father died the next year. The farm was sold and Darlene went to live with her aunt and uncle, her mother's older brother and his wife and family.

"I found a haven in the horses and living in the country. I went for walks all the time," she said. "Between those two things I maintained my sanity. Horses, of course, were my life. I'd come home from school, get my snack, go to the barn and be there until nine o'clock at night. That's where my friends were. Anything outside the barn, I was a basket case."

Close to a straight 4.0 student in high school with a strong independent streak, Sandlin said she would get tough on herself if she received any grade other than an A. That carried over to college. She graduated from the University of Missouri in Kansas City, a 3.83 grade point average in business, with a concentration in finance.

It was during college that Sandlin was, for really the first time, without a horse in her life. She had sold the junior hunter she had been showing, bought a car and gone to college.

"It was very difficult," she said. "I couldn't look at a horse. I couldn't go to a horse show. I missed it so much that I kept myself away.

"I wanted to do well in school. What I thought I should do was quit riding, go to school, get a good job and ride for fun on the side, and be satisfied with that even though deep down my dreams were always to ride for the Team, to show internationally, to go to the Olympics. All of these were my dreams, but for whatever reason, I made myself believe that it would be more sensible to get a real job, to live the life of a normal person. I was trying to be very practical. Who knows why?"

Then Sandlin got married. At twenty. She was ready to be the perfect Junior Leaguer, banker, a wife with a husband and a house on the lake.

Somewhere, the practical side of Sandlin took a vacation. She began riding again. In 1986 she bought Basil, a well-traveled jumper.

"That was the beginning of the end or the beginning of the beginning, who knows what you want to call it. I wanted to go show and my husband didn't understand it."

They divorced.

Somewhere, somehow, when Sandlin decided to let horses back into her life, she, at the same time, let go of the image of herself in power suits, doing community service, kids, station wagons and riding just as a hobby.

"I didn't know if I could ever make it unless I tried," she said of her riding. "I decided to try, to wing it."

Within a week of graduation, she was training with Wilson Dennahey in Denver.

"I was twenty-two, and I wanted to go for it. I had this image in my mind of what I should be and that's what I thought I had to live up to. But it wasn't an image I fit into. I have no idea where that image came from. I tried to be that type, I tried really hard for a while, but it didn't work."

Since then, the riding life of Darlene Sandlin was one of peaks and valleys . . . like the rest of life, she said.

"What can I say? I'm doing exactly what I've always wanted to do. I'm living out the dream I always had. I'm very happy with it. Every day I appreciate it. Every time I get to ride an extra horse I appreciate it. Every time I go in the show ring, especially when I win, I appreciate it."

After the victory, the ribbon presentation and the press conference someone mentioned to Sandlin that she had arrived, that she was a star.

"I don't want to be a star," she said. "I just want to be part of the team."

After, wearing a long, brown waxed-cotton duster, Sandlin walked up the ramp from the arena to the stabling area. Her helmet still on, flowers still cradled in her arm, one hand holding onto the gold medal around her neck, Sandlin walked slowly. She wasn't tired. It was a leisurely stroll. Sandlin took her time, making the night last a little longer, basking in its glow.

The next day Sandlin was in a photo session when a group of 4-H kids from Connecticut walked by.

"Who's that?" one of them asked.

"Darlene Sandlin."

"Who?"

While she was at first unrecognizable, Sandlin soon made herself unforgettable to the gaggle of 4-H kids at the National. For the next half hour, Sandlin answered questions from the young riders. She signed autographs on programs, on scraps of paper, even on the T-shirt of one boy.

"Would you like to meet my horse?" she asked.

Sandlin then led the somewhat startled group of 4-Hers and their leaders toward the stabling area, chatting all the way. She retrieved Alley Oop from the quarantine area reserved for international riders, and held the big Belgian Warmblood for the kids to pet.

Riding, at any level, is about the bond between horse and rider. The one between Sandlin and Alley Oop goes beyond that, is deeper. She wanted him to share in the adulation of the 4-H kids.

The day before a grand prix in Minnesota several years ago, Sandlin added up her bills. The total was more than she had.

"I told him we had to win," she said. "And he understood. I know he did. No question." And he did.

One leader was nonplussed by the impromptu clinic and the friendliness of the young woman in the red jacket. The woman finally insisted the children thank Sandlin and leave.

Watching them walk away, Sandlin was clearly amazed. She shook her head, smiled, as much the beneficiary of the encounter as the 4-Hers from Connecticut.

*   *   *

For Michael, the National was a success. A somewhat unexpected one. He rode in one class, the $100,000 AGA Championship, and won it. Michael didn't have to show through the week, spend time in the parking-lot-turned-stabling-area, or rise early and stay late to school horses. He wasn't there coaching students.

Instead, he flew in from Lexington, Kentucky, where he had attended the Breeder's Cup races the day before to ride a well-rested Heisman, who, like Michael, had been spared the grinding schedule of indoors. Lisa Jacquin had schooled Heisman.

Heisman was in fine form that day. Michael and the big chestnut went twelfth in the field of sixteen, and became one of six to go clear and make it to the jump-off.

Silver Skates, the mare, new to Katie Monahan Prudent in Tampa when the pair barely qualified for the American Invitational in March, was clear at 38.111 seconds in the jump-off. They were followed by Tony Font and Lego, who had 8 faults. Debbie Shaffner and Volan had 4.

Then it was Michael's turn. He and Heisman were clear, and trimmed more than two seconds off the time of Monahan Prudent and Silver Skates. They were far from in the clear. To follow were two of the best horse-rider combinations of the year.

Jacquin, like Michael, went clear, but a little more than half a second off her mentor's pace. Likewise, Goldstein and Saluut II were also clear but about a second slower still.

A year ago, Michael had sat in the stands of the Meadowlands and watched. Even late in this season he had spoken as if he had no intention of taking part in any of the indoors shows. He disliked the grind, the difficulty, the excessive demand on the horses.

But, in the end, Sale Johnson, Heisman's owner, convinced him to give it a shot. He won the AGA Championship. In the process, he was able to announce that 1992 could be a possible Olympic year for him and Heisman or maybe Rhum IV.

As much as he savored the year-ending victory, Michael strode hurriedly through the arena to meet the press. He was anxious to avoid the inevitable traffic backup that was about to occur as the Giants game ended at the nearby stadium.

*   *   *

The National Horse Show was once again living up to its name. The scar that was the 1990 show had healed. It had been an exciting six days, one of spotlights and celebrities and parties, and even a U.S. victory in the Nations Cup.

A year before, Hap Hansen had sped from the arena at the Meadowlands behind the wheel of a bright red Cadillac Allanté, the spoils of Rider of the Year honors. This year he had watched from crutches, an ankle injured in a riding accident relegating him to spectatorship. Goldstein, ever aggressive, was Rider of the Year for 1991, driving off the Allanté.

A year before, Tony Font won the show's final big class, and Lego was Horse of the Year. This year, the amiable Texan made it to the jump-off and settled for a smaller slice of pie. Lego, at the same time, was for sale. The Goldstein-Jacquin race came down to the final class, with For The Moment walking off with Horse of the Year honors in 1991.

A year ago, Tracey Feeney hadn't even been at the National. This year she was, but only after the horse trailer she had been towing from Dallas caught fire and burned. The horses were saved, but not her clothes or tack, and she showed in her first East Coast indoors wearing borrowed clothes.

Still, Hansen and Feeney were at the National. They, like Kate and Beezie and Goldstein and Fargis and Font and Jacquin and the others, had been drawn here. To some, it didn't make economic sense; this is an expensive place to show, but they came. To some, it didn't make any kind of sense; this was the tail end of a grueling season, but they too came.

No, the Meadowlands wasn't the Garden, but this still was the National.

In the end, 66,941 spectators—including the Girl Scouts and school kids—had watched the 108th edition of the National Horse Show. That was 30 percent more than a year before.

Then, the society orchestra packed up and gone, the last rustle of gowns a mere memory and merchants in the mezzanine shopping area straggling out, a man piloted a massive yellow front-loader across the area that less than an hour before had been the holding area between the warmup ring and the in-gate. In powerful mechanized bites, the foot of dirt that had been laid down was coming up. It was being loaded into a dump truck and hauled away. The Brendan Byrne Arena was being turned back to basketball and hockey players.

In the stabling area, tractor-trailers and two-horse trailers alike ebbed out of the parking lot. Some were bound for Toronto and the Royal Winter Fair, others were simply heading home, a brief rest before heading to Florida, where the media circus that would be known as the William Kennedy Smith rape trial became the latest obsession of CNN.

Not far from where Smith was on trial, the tribulation of the Palm Beach Polo and Country Club was temporarily resolved. Federal bankruptcy judge Falcon Hawkins ruled in favor of the club's bankruptcy petition. So, when the Winter Equestrian Festival opened in January, it would open at a facility protected from its creditors and the federal Resolution Trust Corporation.

CHAPTER 14

Home for Christmas

It was a wonderful rumor. However, that's all it was, one of those drips of conversation that becomes a tidal wave rushing toward a landfall of truth and never making it.

Somehow, sometime after the National, John was supposed to have purchased Gem Twist for $3 million. John was surprised to hear the news. As surprised as Frank Chapot, Gem's trainer, who called to inquire about what he had heard.

The rumor started, it seems, from an interview Gem's owner, Michael Golden, did with Nancy Jaffer in which he said he was putting the horse on the market. He was discouraged by what had happened in the sport in the short while he had been involved, and saw the objective criteria for Team selection as the biggest of all problems.

With that shred, someone linked the Moons. It then became that the Moons bought Gem Twist for Beezie to take her shot at the Olympics.

Not so.

But in the comparatively idle days before Christmas, John had returned from yet another quick horse-shopping trip to Europe. Nothing had come of that either.

He sat in the kitchen of his home in Cazenovia, a thin coverlet of snow on the hilly central New York countryside. A fire in the cast-iron

187

kitchen stove crackled, and John finished a follow-up phone call with Johan Heins in De Wijk, Holland.

John and his mother went two out of three good-natured verbal falls on topics as diverse as the William Kennedy Smith trial and deposed White House Chief of Staff John Sununu. Terry and Beezie came in from working the horses. In a busy year, it took until almost Christmas for everyone to be home and anchored.

John had flown to Europe nearly a dozen times during the year and had just returned from an extensive two-week trip to South America. Most of the time, he was trying to find horses for clients. He also sold two horses to European owners and bought a couple for himself. It had been a year of a lot more work for a lot fewer sales. Fortunately, said John, all were sizable deals.

That was a commentary on the year as a whole. Back in Florida, Beezie and John said it would be a year of consolidation, one to concentrate on the business side of things. Much of this had to do with the calendar. It was not a year with major international events, no World Championships, no Olympics, and this affected the feel of the entire year.

For Beezie, it was a year of working hard to stay in the thick of things. Certainly, Prost's numerous wins in speed classes were a bright spot. Also, Beezie and Schnapps wound up eighteenth on the IBM/USET computer listing. And there had been real progress by the amateurs riding with her and John, and that was something they had wanted to accomplish. In Florida, Beezie and John had talked about this being a year of consolidation, of building.

As for the year ahead, "the jury is still out," said John, and Beezie agreed. Ping Pong, one of the horses Harry Gill had placed with them, if he progressed, could do well. Also, Beanbag, another of Gill's horses, was coming out of retirement and Beezie would be riding him.

Yet, with questions of Florida waiting to be answered, the Olympic trials were still in a mist. There was no one super horse with Beezie's name on it.

A few days later, Beezie flew to Wisconsin to spend the holiday with her parents before joining the southerly migration of the Northeast's horse community. It had been just such a Christmas years earlier when all of this began. The horses, the travel, the training, the riding, the ceremony all began with that Christmas pony appearing in the driveway of the family home in Wisconsin.

*   *   *

Counting fruit flies with curly wings paid off. Kate got a B in her genetics class. Then she found out she might need yet another class for one of the vet schools to which she continued to apply. So she enrolled for the spring semester at Vanderbilt for the one class. Instead of commuting between home, Brown University and horse shows, she could fly from the winter shows in Florida to Nashville. Kate Chope, Frequent Flyer.

In between the National and heading south to ride again, Kate was forced to put down an old friend. Tattersall, a mare that had been her small junior hunter horse, colicked badly. Despite the best efforts of veterinarians at Tufts, the mare had to be euthanized. Left behind, however, was a five-month-old filly, JoJo, an offspring of the mare and Sebastian.

It had been a year to grow on. She had wanted to set aside the analysis and the pretty picture of the proper equitation rider and develop confidence, ride on instinct.

Goldstein, the perfect model for that, said Kate had succeeded. Confidence grew with every round. Ginsing had been the right choice, a horse capable of rattling a fence or two or three and still finishing the course, so Kate got saddle time in big classes with big jumps and big-name riders. Had he been too careful, he'd have lost confidence, and Kate would not have gained hers.

Reiten lernt Man nur durch reiten, read a sign on the wall of Paul Stecken's stable in Munster, Westphalia. "You learn to ride only by riding."

Kate did.

She also learned about herself.

After Washington and before the National, Kate caught herself thinking, "Wow, I could do this and only this full time forever." She had ridden confidently at Harrisburg, done well at Washington, including the puissance, and returning to the National always heightened her excitement. She had found a rhythm, grown into the big classes, spent enough time immersed in the horse-show world to become part of it, a real part, and not a young rider who came in to show on the weekends and left. "Then I thought, wait, vet school."

Kate had stepped beyond the amateur classes. Moreover, she had woven herself deeper into the very fabric of the show world. Professionals commented and complimented her on her rounds. She came to know more people and became comfortable with the ebb and flow of life on the road. It had been, as she realized on her drive from Tallahassee to Houston eight months earlier, a dream year, one to remember.

*   *   *

For Michael, it had been a good year. He had won three grand prix—Kings Mill, Mexico City and the AGA Championship at the National—and got a piece of numerous others. He had been as consistent as he had wanted to be, and Heisman had proved himself. Once again, wins at Devon and the American Invitational escaped him, but in the end those were minor in comparison to all the good that had gone on.

D. D. had an outstanding Florida, winning her first grand prix riding Tashiling, and qualifying for the American Invitational. She rode for the Team at the Pan American Games. Dina Santangelo almost made it to Havana.

Jacquin and For The Moment had some outstanding moments of their own. He was Horse of the Year. They won at Gladstone and spent the entire season on a seesaw with Goldstein.

But, more than anything, the year offered some credence to a casual remark Michael had made one day sitting in his office at his Vintage Farm.

"Maybe I've got one more Olympics in me," he had said.

With Heisman performing the way he had, and Michael announcing at the Gladstone Festival of Champions that Rhum IV was his new Jet Run, it seemed as though he could have another run at an Olympic gold medal.

About the time the Winter Equestrian Festival would get underway in earnest, Michael would celebrate his forty-first birthday. But, in general, in show jumping that is not old, and the man was in excellent physical condition. Michael Matz in the red coat and blue collar of the USET at Barcelona, that alone was enough to make many forget the dismal showing of Americans abroad during 1991.

And maybe, just maybe, his luck at the American Invitational would change. After all, the show in November announced it was leaving Tampa Stadium and setting up shop in the new Sun Coast Dome in St. Petersburg.

*   *   *

After the National, Goldstein, Alice Debany, Darlene Sandlin and Michael Dorman rode for the USET at the Royal Winter Fair in Toronto, one of North America's truly memorable equine events. They finished third in the Nations Cup, and second in the competition for Leading Team honors. The performance at Toronto made the USET's record for indoors much better than last year. The USET had been the Leading Team at Washington and New York and won the Nations Cup at the National. A year earlier, the only honor was Leading Team at the National.

For those kindly disposed to the IBM/USET computer ranking used to select team members, the Team's performance in 1991 was evidence in its favor. Last year, the criterion had been money won. This year, science stepped in.

Also at Toronto, Goldstein and Daydream, and Turi and Ever If Ever repeated their puissance rivalry. They tied at 7′ 5″, being paid a bonus for the last two rounds of the class. The finish made Daydream the first horse in USET history to sweep the puissance at all three indoors shows, Washington, New York and Toronto.

For Goldstein, it had been a year similar to the name of her puissance horse, a Daydream. She won eight grand prix, the most ever by one rider. She had as strong a string of horses as any rider, and she worked hard, showed often and traveled extra miles to ride. As the year wound down, she was nominated as the AHSA's Equestrian of the Year.

"Maybe it was a little bit of being hungry, having missed so much of the year before," said Goldstein. "Maybe the horses were rested because of last year. Whatever it was, everything just seemed to come together."

Indoors had been a respite for Goldstein. Two or three rides a day.

However, the week after Toronto signaled a return to the routine that had, over the years, made all the rest possible. Goldstein was back in Florida riding forty to fifty horses a day, many of which she hadn't even seen in six months. She took Christmas week off, but was back to the routine soon after.

Still, the plan for 1992 was to be vastly different from the one for the year that was ending. Goldstein said Saluut II would rest, not showing until Tampa. He'd be conserved, saving his significant power for the Olympic trials in May and June.

Lisa Jacquin, who with one horse, For The Moment, had challenged Goldstein and her lineup of power hitters for the top spot on the IBM/ USET computer ranking, set her sights in a similar way. All season long she believed the aging Thoroughbred had one more Olympics in him.

*   *   *

All rumors aside, Greg Best finished the year in about as fine a way as anyone can: in Hawaii. He spent a couple weeks there giving lessons and clinics. It was an encore to a visit he had made in April. That time he had judged a show and then done clinics.

"I said let's do it the other way around next time," he said.

He was pleased with the results of his December trip. Students he had worked with were either champion or reserve champion in the classes they entered.

Of nearly equal importance was the fact that Best broke 90 on the golf links for the first time. The last four days of his stay, Best played two courses each day. In the afternoon, midway through this golf marathon, he scored 89 for eighteen holes.

From Hawaii, Best returned home and promptly headed south. Taken with him to Florida was a fifteen-page document, a sponsorship agreement between him and Budweiser. He was reading it a final time before signing it.

So, the new season would begin with the Budweiser logo appearing on all of Best's saddlepads and show announcers introducing him as riding "Budweiser Gem Twist," just as they used to call the gelding "Moët et Chandon Gem Twist" when Best was sponsored by the French champagne maker.

This was the deal that had started back when Best was a spectator at the Michelob American Invitational in Tampa in March. It had been nursed along during the year and finally agreed upon.

"I'm pleased for a lot of reasons," Best said. "It's a big step anytime anything like this brings more corporate attention to the sport. It's good for me and I think it's good for other riders, it opens more opportunities for them."

Ironically, it would be yet another Budweiser horse—a reprise of the day of Miss Budweiser—in the Olympics if Best's goals for 1992 were to come true.

*   *   *

For Sandlin, it seemed the National would have been enough. Hardly.

Toronto turned out to be her best show of the year. She won an open jumper class, was second in another and posted one clear and one 4-fault round in the Nations Cup. To make the victory that much nicer, Sandlin's boyfriend—whose Navy pilot's wings she wears under her red coat when she's in the ring—arrived the day she won.

But it didn't stop there.

On the one day off she had while in Toronto, she and Dorman and

Ronnie Beard went to Peter Stoeckl's farm to look at horses. It was there that she saw a five-year-old Dutch-bred, a horse "as much like Alley Oop as any I've ever seen."

But as much as Sandlin liked the horse, buying it was just not in the cards. That is, until her two older sisters informed her that they would help make the purchase possible. One loaned Sandlin the money for the purchase. The other became part owner.

"I knew they supported me and my riding," she said. "But it's a different kind of support when they do something like that."

So, when Sandlin headed to Florida, it was with a new horse, one that she said was "very green but can jump the moon." She planned to start him in the low preliminaries or schooling jumpers in Florida, but not before a name change.

Three woman had been partners in the horse before, naming him Let's Go Dutch. Sandlin was looking for something different, something befitting the horse's athleticism that was so strong, so powerful, that he made the jumping look effortless.

Sandlin's boyfriend told her about an article he had read in an aviation journal. It was about a new jet that is so powerful it doesn't need after-burners to reach Mach speed. He told her the flight in this new jet was called "super cruise."

As a result, Super Cruise, all 16.3 hands of him and growing, joined Alley Oop and TNT.

"He's great," she said. "The year was great. The only thing I can think of in the last six months that wasn't, was having my wisdom teeth out at Christmas."

*   *   *

Another young rider, David Raposa, wasn't able to repeat the winning he had done in 1990. However, it was a banner year for the sale of horses, something on which he had come to concentrate. War and recession aside, Raposa had made money selling horses, especially during Florida. Even riders as talented as Raposa cannot live alone on the winnings of the horses they ride.

*   *   *

Katie Monahan was back. The 1991 show-jumping season had settled that. The pregnancy. The accident. The recovery. All of those were behind her. Special Envoy had been sold, and other of her horses were injured. But Silver Skates had proven to be worth its weight in gold. Katie had a grand prix victory in the year, and several finishes in the good ribbons.

Husband Henri had seen his horse The King sold. However, he still won a big class at the National.

Besides, the two had traveled the circuit with their son, Adam, a two-year-old bundle of energy and smiles.

*   *   *

As the year ended, Tommy Burns was scheduled for trial in late January. Just shy of a year since Streetwise was injured and had to be put down, the Florida Department of Agriculture and Consumer Affairs was all but done with the case. By mid-January, Burns decided to change his plea from innocent.

Not done, however, was the federal probe. As horsemen rested after the demands of the season, an assistant U.S. attorney in Chicago was looking into the matter.

Rumors went through the show-jumping community like a devastating case of strangles. The names of several prominent trainers and riders surfaced in connection with the probe. It seemed as though those names might eventually appear on future indictments. From a violation of Florida agricultural law, the death of Streetwise had become a high-profile— including a segment on Geraldo Rivera's talk show—nationwide investigation of high-stakes insurance fraud. It had become one with career-ending implications for a number of people if you believed even a part of the speculation.

*   *   *

In France, Jappeloup died. After a triumphant farewell tour of ten selected shows, the smallish, French-bred black jumper retired in September. He died of heart failure November 5.

*   *   *

As the year unwound, the Palm Beach Polo and Country Club continued to operate under the shield of federal bankruptcy law. The Resolution Trust Corporation worked to see that reversed, but as preparations began for the opening of the Winter Equestrian Festival at the end of January, the resort remained sheltered from takeover by the government.

*　　*　　*

Other financial troubles outside the horse industry caused some tense moments within it. The Persian Gulf War, the recession, America's changing taste combined to spell disaster for the sales of Johnny Walker Black Label Scotch, the $1 million sponsor of the AGA show-jumping circuit.

Because of major sales losses, the company decided to pull out. Not only did they cease their sponsorship of the events, but also their backing of Debbie Shaffner. However, she was signed by Manna-Pro, a horse feed. One use of grain for another.

Just as Sallie Wheeler stepped in to save the National, the company that made hers the royal family of St. Louis filled the sponsorship gap of American show jumping. The move was not without a tinge of irony. In 1950 August Busch purchased the mare Circus Rose at the National, renamed her Miss Budweiser and loaned the horse to the USET. This bit of commercialism was then frowned upon by the international show-jumping community, which today sees horses with corporate sponsor names affixed to their names, jump standards shaped like beer and Scotch bottles, and corporate logos stitched to riders' saddlepads.

However, luring those corporate dollars to Del Mar and the latest American staging of the Volvo World Cup Finals was proving difficult, as the event loomed just five months away. The recession played a part in this problem. So did the fact that the America's Cup 12-meter yacht races were scheduled for San Diego about the same time, siphoning off some of the sponsors seeking upscale customers.

Brooks Perry, chairman of the committee staging the competition at the venerable California racetrack, had been at the National two years running, touting the show. Her mission in 1990 was to whip up support for the event, and in 1991 it was to convince people that the World Cup Finals would indeed take place. She came armed with a videotape showing work on the arena covering, since rumors were rampant that it wouldn't be done in time.

Still, rumors persisted as the year ended.

*　　*　　*

It was more than just rumors that swirled around the USET after one of its most tumultuous years had ended. It seemed another was about to begin.

The indoors season had been good: leading team at Washington and New York and second in Toronto, a Nations Cup win in New York. But those horse-show successes faded in the face of a proxy fight over control of the USET.

In late December Charles Dolan, father of show jumper Debbie Dolan, informed the Team that he was mounting a proxy fight. He intended to solicit votes from USET members for a slate of officers other than the one being nominated by the Team at its annual meeting to be held in Florida in late January. A letter was sent to members over the names of show jumpers Joe Fargis, Armand Leone, Jr., and Conrad Homfeld. They had asked to have the proxies returned to them, proxies that would be exercised at the annual meeting to elect new officers.

It was a first. It was an expensive first. Attorneys specializing in proxy fights do not come cheaply, an expense that was especially hard to swallow in light of the Olympic excursion just seven months off. It would add to the existing legal bills brought on by Dolan's earlier lawsuit, the appeal of which was expected to be heard in about two months.

*   *   *

In the end, the span of time between the National Horse Shows of 1990 and 1991 was a trying one for American show jumping. It was a good time too.

The sport began in earnest to wrestle with the problems of maturity, of becoming a business and not a pastime. Lawsuits crept into the sport the way they had in baseball, football and other games. Sponsorships came and went. It remained a most dangerous sport, but still one with mandated headgear more stylish than safe. The computerized rating system continued to draw the ire of many, the laughter of others and a task force to study how it could be improved. Some shows flourished. Some sought ways to stay afloat. One, the Children's Services charity show held in May in Farmington, Connecticut, announced it was moving across the border to Paul Greenwood's Old Salem Farm.

And the National seemed once again to be the National Horse Show. One show does not a return to greatness make. However, the 1991 version showed what's possible.

"It was a much happier show than the year before," said Hank Collins. "Everyone seemed pleased with how it went: exhibitors, spectators and sponsors."

In one of the most important criteria of all, early indications were that the show made money, something Sallie Wheeler called amazing.

"All the bills aren't in, but I think we've made enough to make us feel comfortable," said Wheeler. "I think too that we're in a position to make money from now on."

While many exhibitors credited Wheeler directly with the turnaround, Wheeler was quick to spread around the praises.

"I thought that it was the National again," said Wheeler.

*   *   *

Finally, Tony Font made the trip back to Texas, two-horse trailer behind his pickup. He had made this drive and others like it countless times, but this time he was heading home to Houston to a new prospect. The reams of paperwork had finally ended, and financing was in place for the barn that would give him greater independence.

It would be modest. It would include an apartment in the barn rather than a house. It would have twelve stalls and work areas. Still, it was a major step, one of permanence, one that would allow him to develop clients of his own, give lessons, accept more horses for training.

Building the barn took on added significance. After the National, the Font-Lego partnership dissolved. Bob Lemmons placed the horse at a farm in Oklahoma to be sold, not campaigned, just sold.

The year had been a solid year for Font and Lego. They didn't win any grand prix, but had good ribbons in several, including a fine performance in the American Invitational. They were always there, always a threat in any jump-off they made. Lego had been hurt twice, taking about a two-month bite out of the middle of the season, and depriving him of a chance to ride in Havana.

"This year couldn't compare to 1990," Font said. "But I knew that in 1990. That was the best year that horse ever had and probably ever will have."

The loss of Lego put a new importance on the construction project and on his business as a whole. He had done some clinics after the National, and having a place of his own would allow for more, as well as teaching, and sales. Font still planned to go to Arizona, this time with some green horses, and nothing like Lego, no special horse for special classes.

"I've had to start over before," said Font. "No horse ever lasts forever."

Index